155.3   12,078
McC

   McCuen, Gary E.
   THE SEXUAL REVOLUTION: TRADITION
AL MORES VERSUS NEW VALUES.

DATE DUE		
~~DEER~~ ~~MAR 1 8~~		
~~MAR 2 5~~ OCT-3 1 1997		
~~SEP 1 6~~ NOV 1 8 1998		
~~FOSTER~~		
~~ENG 10~~		
~~ENG 10~~		
~~GRIFFITH~~		
~~ENG 1~~		
~~ENG 10~~		
~~ENG 1~~		
~~HANABY~~		
~~ENG 10~~		

THE SEXUAL REVOLUTION

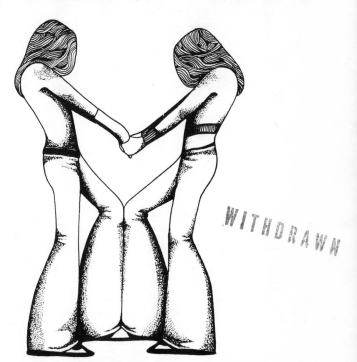

WITHDRAWN

TRADITIONAL MORES VERSUS NEW VALUES

12,078

GARY E. McCUEN
DAVID L. BENDER
(Editors)

Greenhaven Press Inc. — 1611 Polk St. N.E., Mpls., MN 55413

© COPYRIGHT 1972 by GREENHAVEN PRESS
ISBN 0-912616-12-1 Paper Edition
ISBN 0-912616-31-8 Cloth Edition

TABLE OF CONTENTS

TABLE OF CONTENTS

TABLE OF EXERCISES

A major emphasis of this book is on critical thinking skills. Discussion exercises included after readings are not laborious writing assignments. They are written only to stimulate class discussion and individual critical thinking.

IS THE FAMILY OBSOLETE?

THE FAMILY IS DEAD

by Ferdinand Lundberg*

Ferdinand Lundberg was born in Chicago and practiced journalism there and in New York. His experience as a financial journalist and his studies in philosophy and sociology led to many best selling books, including **Imperial Hearst, America's Sixty Families** and **Modern Woman: The Lost Sex.** He has written many articles for numerous magazines and journals and has been a Professor of Social Philosophy at New York University.

Consider the following questions while reading:

1. For what reasons does the author feel that the family is near the point of complete extinction?
2. The author claims that the pre-industrial family and the modern family were held together by similar forces. Do you agree with his analysis?
3. What are some of the problems experienced in modern families?

*From **The Coming World Transformation** by Ferdinand Lundberg copyright © 1963 by Ferdinand Lundberg. Reprinted by permission of Doubleday & Company, Inc.

The family as an institution is in fact near the point of complete extinction.

Until the Industrial Revolution the family was the central institution of society — its basic unit of economic production, the principal ground of what little formal education and individual correction there was, the chief center of amusement and recreation, the hospital, the nursing and retirement home for the ailing and the aged, and the smallest unit of local government. Whatever insight it lacked into more cosmic matters was supplied to it by religion. It has been stripped of all these inner functions by technological advance and is increasingly losing residual functions such as food processing and pre-school care of children. Once extended to include at least three generations and various degrees of collateral relationship usually working and living together, often under a single roof, it is now reduced to what sociologists call a purely nuclear form: young parents and dependent children. At the age of eighteen the children tend to relocate either at college or in jobs, leaving a post-mature couple looking forward to retirement from life in more or less straitened circumstances. We see, then, that today's family is not only nuclear but is largely temporary, lacking in continuity.

The nuclear family, most of its onetime basic functions now performed more efficiently by outside agencies, is the plaything of outside events over which it has no control. And gone is the sense of solidarity peculiar to the extended family. Prior to the Industrial Revolution the family was usually sure, barring natural calamities, of its bare livelihood; under advanced technology it is always under threat of unemployment or unsettling income variation owing to technological improvement or economic  imbalance. Additionally, illness or injury of the breadwinners often threatens loss or contraction of livelihood, and with it loss of ready access to agencies of education, amusement, recreation and medical care. In order to avail itself of services it once generated for itself, now greatly improved in quality, the modern family requires more purchasing power than ever before. But the terms of competition for it are completely out of its control, regulated as they are by a market.

The high divorce rate, now involving about one in every three American marriages, is only a partial index to the difficulty of modern marriage, shorn of most practical functions. An undetermined additional number of couples become emotionally estranged, problems to each other and to children, without seeking divorce. Marriages invariably endure solely on grounds of expediency, duty, or affection. But whereas expediency, a sense of duty, and the law (in about that order) kept the preindustrial family together, the main supports of modern marriage are affection and compatibility, a sense of duty, and expediency — a reversal of order. Affection, it is well recognized, is unstable, varying as personalities develop and conditions change. The sense of duty has waned for many with the decline of community solidarity under the cult of economic individualism. And with few concrete needs being met that cannot be satisfied elsewhere, expediency has come to play little role of support. Divorcing couples, their affection turned to hate or indifference, find it more expedient to go their separate ways. ...

Marriage in preindustrial society was indispensably part of a way of life, alone making possible economic as well as much other necessary activity. It was strongly supported by organized religion and endorsed by all conservatives for the stability it produced. Many children in the presence of a high death rate were a guarantee that society would survive. Although the religious and conservatives tenaciously value marriage, they are now not a little confused because the modern family, far from insuring stability, is itself an unstabilizing factor forcing many changes distasteful to traditionalists.

Although still underwritten by religion and conservatism, the principal external impetus for modern marriage, often entered into by bored and unprepared couples, comes from the commercialized romanticism of films and cheap fiction. There marriage is depicted as a panacea, promising to dissolve all difficulties in sexual gratification. Joined with this cue is the democratic idea that every individual, no matter how unsuited for responsibility, is entitled to a mate and children. As the promised gratification turns out to be less than expected and difficulties intrude from a world of

4

change, many families present themselves, overtly or covertly, as social problems.

Modern marriage, commercially presented as a blissful haven, turns out more often than not to be a joint exercise by two unprepared people in solving an endless series of novel problems. Many find their resilience and resourcefulness limited and at some point break down under the strain.

THE NUCLEAR FAMILY IS DISINTEGRATING

The nuclear family is slowly disintegrating. Men leave because the pressure of supporting a family is too great. Children leave because parents demand too much of them and because they have a higher allegiance to their peers. Women usually suffer in this process. Either they are left to provide financially for their children when the father leaves or they must take on employment in addition to their work at home in order to make ends meet and keep the family together.

The nuclear family must be replaced with a new form of family where individuals live and work together to help to meet the needs of all people in the society. New space must be found to house this family and new collectivized work must prevent members from being exploited and isolated from each other.

Nancy Lehmann and Helen Sullinger in **The Document**.

THE FAMILY IS THE CORNERSTONE OF OUR SOCIETY

by Catholic, Protestant and Jewish groups

This statement was issued jointly in 1966 by the Family Life Bureau of the United States Catholic Conference, the Commission on Marriage and Family of the National Council of the Churches of Christ in the U.S.A. and the Committee on the Family of the Synagogue Council of America.

Use the following questions to assist you in your reading:

1. How do the religious groups which authored this statement believe God plays a role in family life?
2. What is meant by the statement ''the family is the cornerstone of our society?''

Keenly aware of the role religion ascribes to the home and family life and keenly aware of the powerful and pervasive social conditions which threaten to undermine human dignity, marriage and family life in America, we, as representatives of the major religions — Catholic, Jewish, Orthodox, and Protestant — wish to bring the religious teachings of our respective faiths to bear upon our society and to join with all men of good will to create a healthier social climate in which family life in America can flourish and be strong.

There are large areas of agreement and numerous possibilities for joint programs and action, although we recognize and respect the differences of approach, emphasis and contributions of each major faith.

To help families develop foundations for personally meaningful and socially responsible behavior, we offer the following affirmations on which our historic faiths unite.

We believe and unite in affirming, that God, the Creator of the Universe and the Father of all mankind, did create us male and female and did establish families as part of his Divine Plan. Because of our understanding of this plan, we believe and unite in affirming that our sexuality is a wondrous gift from God to be accepted with thanksgiving and used within marriage with reverence and joy.

We believe and unite in affirming that our understanding of God's plan for marriage ideally calls for lifelong commitment in fidelity to a continuing, supportive relationship in which each partner helps the other to develop to fullest capacity. We are united in our belief that God is an active partner in sustaining and enriching the husband-wife relationship in marriage.

We believe and unite in affirming that children are a trust from God and that parenthood is a joyous, though strenuous, adventure in partnership with God for the procreation and nurturing of each child. Parenthood calls for the responsible use of all of our God-given talents and abilities in this adventure.

We believe and unite in affirming that family life is the cradle of personality and character for each child and creates an environment for the societal values of each succeeding generation as well as the principal source of meaningful personal relations for each adult member of our society. All children need a father and a mother firmly united in love to guide their growth into manhood or womanhood and to provide the emotional security that fosters development toward mature and responsible relationships between men and women.

We believe that the family is the cornerstone of our society. It shapes the attitudes, the hopes, the ambitions, the values of every citizen. The child is usually damaged when family living collapses. When this happens on a massive scale, the community itself is crippled.

There are no easy answers to all the complex problems facing marriage and family living in the world today, and we are aware that there are many fronts on which we must work. We can never finish the task; neither are we free to ignore it.

Therefore, we the major religious groups in the U.S., join forces in exploring all ways and means available to preserve and strengthen family life in America to the end that each person may enjoy fulfillment in dignity, justice, and peace.

THE FAMILY WILL SURVIVE

The family — in all man's history — has never been replaced by revolution or impositions from without, nor has it totally disintegrated. Instead, subject to the most disruptive social forces, it has shifted — adapted — and sometimes just waited out the revolution — but it has always found the way to adjust. In the process it has done moderately well for all its members, but like all human institutions, it has hardly ever been perfect. In a less than perfect world, what more should we expect?

Rev. James T. McHugh
Director, Family Life Division
United States Catholic Conference

8

FACT AND OPINION

This discussion exercise is designed to promote experimentation with one's ability to distinguish between fact and opinion. It is a fact, for example, that the United States has been militarily involved in the Vietnam War. But to say this involvement serves the interests of world peace is an opinion or conclusion. Future historians will agree that American soldiers fought in Vietnam, but their interpretations about the causes and consequences of the war will probably vary greatly.

Most of the following statements are taken from the readings in this book and some have other origins. Consider each statement carefully. Mark (O) for any statement you feel is an opinion or interpretation of the facts. Mark (F) for any statement you believe is a fact. Discuss and compare your judgments with those of other class members.

O = OPINION
F = FACT

_____1. The family is near the point of complete extinction.

_____2. The basic functions of today's family are more efficiently performed by outside agencies.

_____3. The family is the cornerstone of our society.

_____4. Good marriages are made in heaven and have God's support.

_____5. Our society could not survive the disintegration of the nuclear family.

_____ 6.   It is more difficult for parents to raise children today than it was for parents in the past.

_____ 7.   Professional parenthood, as recommended in Reading 3, would result in a more stable society.

_____ 8.   The present nuclear family is the best method possible for passing on acceptable moral stand-ards and respect for the law to new generations.

_____ 9.   The advantages of ''cluster group families,'' as described in Reading 5, outweigh the advantages of the nuclear family.

_____10.   The divorce rate in the U.S. is higher now than in the past.

_____11.   American children are given too much freedom and independence.

_____12.   Most church bodies favor the nuclear family over communal living.

PROFESSIONAL PARENTS

by Alvin Toffler*

Alvin Toffler is a former Associate Editor of **Fortune** and has been a Visiting Professor at Cornell University and a Visiting Scholar at the Russell Sage Foundation. His articles have appeared in scholarly journals as well as such varied publications as **Life** and **Playboy**. His books include **The Culture Consumers, The Schoolhouse in The City** and the very popular **Future Shock**.

The following questions should help you examine the reading:

1. What does Toffler mean when he says that "parenthood remains the greatest single preserve of the amateur?"
2. What advantages would professional parenthood have over our present method of raising children?

Bio-Parents and Pro-Parents

If a smaller number of families raise children, however, why do the children have to be their own? Why not a system under which "professional parents" take on the childbearing function for others?

Raising children, after all, requires skills that are by no means universal. We don't let "just anyone" perform brain surgery or, for that matter, sell stocks and bonds. Even the lowest ranking civil servant is required to pass tests proving competence. Yet we allow virtually anyone, almost without regard for mental or moral qualifications, to try his or her hand at raising young human beings, so long as these humans are biological offspring. Despite the increasing complexity of the task, parenthood remains the greatest single preserve of the amateur.

As the present system cracks and the super-industrial revolution rolls over us, as the armies of juvenile delinquents swell, as hundreds of thousands of youngsters flee their homes, and students rampage at universities in all the technosocieties, we can expect vociferous demands for an end to parental dilettantism.

There are far better ways to cope with the problems of youth, but professional parenthood is certain to be proposed, if only because it fits so perfectly with the society's overall push toward specialization. Moreover, there is a powerful, pent-up demand for this social innovation. Even now millions of parents, given the opportunity, would happily relinquish their parental responsibilities — and not necessarily through irresponsibility or lack of love. Harried, frenzied, up against the wall, they have come to see themselves as inadequate to the tasks. Given affluence and the existence of specially-equipped and licensed professional parents, many of today's biological parents would not only gladly surrender their children to them, but would look upon it as an act of love, rather than rejection.

Parental professionals would not be therapists, but actual family units assigned to, and well paid for, rearing children. Such families might be multi-generational by design, offering children in them an opportunity to observe and learn from a variety of adult models, as was the case in the old farm homestead. With the adults paid to be professional parents, they would be freed of the occupational necessity to

12

relocate repeatedly. Such families would take in new children as old ones ''graduate'' so that age-segregation would be minimized.

Thus newspapers of the future might well carry advertisements addressed to young married couples: ''Why let parenthood tie you down? Let us raise your infant into a responsible, successful adult. Class A Pro-family offers: father age 39, mother, 36, grandmother, 67. Uncle and aunt, age 30, live in, hold part-time local employment. Four-child-unit has opening for one, age 6-8. Regulated diet exceeds government standards. All adults certified in child development and management. Bio-parents permitted frequent visits. Telephone contact allowed. Child may spend summer vacation with bio-parents. Religion, art, music encouraged by special arrangement. Five year contract, minimum. Write for further details.''

The ''real'' or ''bio-parents'' could, as the ad suggests, fill the role presently played by interested godparents, namely that of friendly and helpful outsiders. In such a way, the society could continue to breed a wide diversity of genetic types, yet turn the care of children over to mother-father groups who are equipped, both intellectually and emotionally, for the task of caring for kids.

THE FAMILY IS NOT OUTDATED

by Dr. S.R. Laycock*

> Dr. Laycock, who is now deceased, was Dean Emeritus of Education, University of Saskatchewan and was formerly Visiting Professor of Education, University of British Columbia. Dr. Laycock's remarks are taken from his book **Family Living and Sex Education** which was published under the sponsorship of the Sub-Committee on Family Life Education of the Canadian Health Specialists Society.

The family is not outdated

The family is an old institution, almost as old as man himself. Contrary to much popular opinion, the family is not breaking down or becoming out-of-date. Today's family, however, faces a host of problems because of the increasing rate of change in conditions of living due to the explosion of knowledge, technological advances and the growth of automation. The family continues to exist because it meets the needs of three groups — children, adults and society at large. The family:

---

*Dr. S.R. Laycock, **Family Living and Sex Education** (Toronto, Canada: Mil-Mac Publications Ltd., 1967), pp. 8-9. Reprinted with permission.

1. Provides for the reproduction of the race;

2. Passes on the cultural heritage of the group;

3. Provides physical security and protection and the material opportunities for living and growth;

4. Meets the deep emotional needs of both children and adults and provides for their social, spiritual, emotional and intellectual development;

5. Develops in its members socially desirable character traits, acceptable moral and ethical standards, and a respect for law;

6. Develops an orderly system of living among its members with provision for eating, sleeping, going to school, going to work, etc.;

7. Develops sound relationships among the family members and between them and their neighbors near and far.

CLUSTER GROUP FAMILIES

by Margaret Mead*

Dr. Mead is one of the fore-most anthropologists in the country. Her expeditions to New Guinea and Bali during a period of over thirty years have resulted in many books and numerous journal and magazine articles. In addition to many other honors and accomplishments, she is a teacher and a past president of the American Anthropology Association, and currently maintains an office at the American Museum of Natural History in New York City.

As you read try to answer the following questions:

1. What is the author referring to when she suggests a "cluster group community"?
2. What advantages does she see for children who grow up in cluster groups rather than nuclear families?

The development of new designs for living — this, I think, is one of the most urgent needs today. We need to look ahead and plan for ways in which families can live that are more in accord with the changes emerging in our society. Above all we must find ways of breaking out of the isolation in which each small family — parents and their small children — still is expected to live. ...

There is the great danger that blind attachment to a traditional kind of family as the only good way of living and bringing up children may in the end frustrate our most serious efforts to improve the quality of our personal and national life. ...

By holding on to a style of family living that has become incongruous with our newer expectations, we shall have lost what we have most valued: a way of bringing up children that prepares them to live their own lives, to make the future their own — and different from the past.

Is there an alternative?

I think there is.

In the past Americans were willing to work very hard for a better life for their children. Significantly, the forms that the "better life" should take seldom were spelled out. Instead, people concentrated on creating the conditions in which a better life was possible and on rearing children who could make innovations in the style of living appropriate to their own generation. This still should be our goal.

Our more immediate aim, I believe, should be the development of a setting in which each family would retain its identity but in which each would be an integral part of a larger group, all of whose members would carry some responsibility for everyone within it, adult or child, man or woman. Because such a group would be complexly organized, it also would be complexly related to the larger community.

In fact, such groups already exist in embryonic form here and there around the country. As far as I know, they have no formal organization or even a descriptive name. I have thought of them — and so I shall call them — as "cluster groups." What I shall describe here is nowhere the reality. It is an ideal picture based on fragments that are as yet only possibilities.

In a cluster community, couples with children would live very close to many people. There would be in each cluster some families, some childless married couples, older and younger, some individuals not yet married, some previously married, some working or studying and some retired, some with strength for energetic play and talk with children and some very fragile persons whom even children could help care for.

In such communities children would come to know adults who differed in their personalities and interests. The only child would have the warm companionship of other children, and no child would be dependent on parents alone as adult models or on one parent to carry all adult responsibilities. The experience of "mine" and "thine" would be modified by both the difficulties and the rewards of interdependence. Some things would be owned personally; other necessary resources would be owned and used within the larger group.

Clusters of this kind should not have a common occupational or economic base. A nationally guaranteed annual income would enable very young people — students and others — along with the elderly and with mothers who choose homemaking and child care as preferred activities, to join clusters of their own choice. But differentiations would continue to be made between working relationships established in the larger community and relationships of love and friendship within the cluster. By having a working life outside, each adult would become a link between "home" and the larger world.

Nor should famlies and individuals necessarily make long-term commitments to membership. It is necessary, I think, for people to keep the sense that they are free to change and move. Only so can they feel that the choices they make carry with them personal responsibility. Americans are easily put off by things they "have to do"; feeling that one has elected a course of action can carry one through many difficulties. ...

Americans have overvalued personal autonomy and independence. Bringing up children within the isolated nuclear family, we can do little else. Growing up instead within cluster groups, children would experience new forms of interdependence and responsiveness so much needed in the modern world. But they would still wean themselves from their particular families, and leaving childhood attachments behind, would make their own way and form new deep and personal attachments.

18

How can we make a beginning?

On the whole, I think experimentation with new styles of living should be voluntary and carried out by groups whose members care about the development of new social forms. There is no use waiting for special facilities to be built. Those who want to try out some form of cluster living will have to make do with what they can find. Large old houses, converted apartment buildings, summer cottages — all these have possibilities.

But this would not be enough. Very small communities might be too ephemeral and some cluster groups might develop the cultlike characteristics of a group made up of over-committed enthusiasts.

We also need experimentation that will draw on the talents of architects, social planners and other experts from the beginning. There is one setting very appropriate for the development of cluster groups. This is the academic community. In every part of the country new educational facilities are springing up, and old ones are being transformed. Within short periods the numbers of students leap from hundreds to thousands. Almost everywhere there is a drastic shortage of housing.

Moreover, we are rapidly approaching the situation in which people from adolescence to retirement will be inter- mittently involved in some form of education or special training. A man or a woman may come to a university for a summer refresher course or settle down for a stay of five or even ten years. But after a certain period all students expect to move on. Many would be willing, even eager, to try out an unfamiliar style of living. ...

In an academic community the members of a cluster might include boys and girls away from home for the first time, married students with and without babies, grandmothers who enjoy young people, young instructors and scholars from distant lands. One cluster might be made up entirely of academics. Another might bring together town and gown. A third might be made up of people from different institutions — space scientists, musicians from a symphony orchestra and zoologists from a field laboratory. No two would be alike. Bridging time and space and areas of knowledge, children and adults living together in such a cluster might learn to see past and future through one another's eyes as they shared the present.

No one can predict the outcome of experiments with new designs for living. Children who had grown up in cluster groups would have a very different view of what they might become from the view we are able to have today, thinking about their possibilities within the framework of our experience of living each in our own separate family home. Clusters would be built on trust in our children's ability to make their own choices for the future.

PREDICTING AND EVALUATING RESPONSES

Much is made of the generation gap, one cause of which is the tendency of young and old to value actions and goals differently. This exercise provides the opportunity to discuss, analyze, and predict how the generations (let us cite two for the purpose of discussion, those over thirty, and those under thirty) would construct different value scales from the same set of choices.

From the following list of choices, list the five you believe the younger generation values most, assigning the number (1) to the choice you believe it would consider most important, and so on, until you have completed five choices. Rank five choices for the older generation also. Discuss your rankings with the class. Give your reasoning for the choices you have made and listen to the reasons your classmates present for the choices they have made.

(A)   Observance of traditional sexual customs

(B)   A childless marriage

(C)   A happy marriage

(D)   A satisfying sex life

(E)   Concern about how outsiders judge their relationships with members of the opposite sex

(F)   Acceptance of homosexuals living together

(G)   Virginity before marriage

(H)   Marriage with a large family

(I)   Complete openness with one's marriage partner

(J)   Self satisfaction in a love relationship

(K)   Primary concern for the loved one's feelings and well being as opposed to self's

(L)   Consideration of involvement in a communal marriage

YOUNGER GENERATION

1st choice _____ why?
2nd choice _____ why?
3rd choice _____ why?
4th choice _____ why?
5th choice _____ why?

OLDER GENERATION

1st choice _____ why?
2nd choice _____ why?
3rd choice _____ why?
4th choice _____ why?
5th choice _____ why?

2 CHAPTER

DO WOMEN NEED LIBERATING?

A FEMINIST MANIFESTO

by Nancy Lehmann & Helen Sullinger*

Ms. Lehmann and Ms. Sullinger are active participants in the Women's Liberation Movement. Both are currently working in Minneapolis, Minnesota.

Bring the following questions to your reading:
1. What is the main point made in this reading?
2. What specific examples are offered as proof?

*Taken from **The Document: Declaration of Feminism** by Nancy Lehmann and Helen Sullinger, undated. This document can be obtained by sending $ .50 to ''The Document'', c/o Nancy Lehmann and Helen Sullinger, P.O. Box 7064, Powderhorn Station, Minneapolis, Minnesota 55407.

A MAN CAN WORK FROM SUN TO SUN BUT A WOMAN'S WORK IS NEVER DONE

The enslavement of women by men was the first form of oppression to appear in human history. It has existed in every type of economic system. ...

For centuries men have used women for their own pleasure and for procreation. Women in all cultures have been primarily, if not solely, responsible for maintaining the life of the human race while men have been gradually leading us all toward self-destruction. ...

Heterosexual relationships are by their very nature oppressive to women in a male dominated society. In Western society sexual roles are defined for the benefit of men. The woman is treated as a sexual object, a thing which exists for the gratification of man to ensure his physical comfort and his sexual pleasure. In the eyes of men this is woman's place — for Eve was created from Adam's rib — or so the story goes.

The single woman is commodity on an open market — available prey for any man. In marriage woman is bought by one man and promised protection from the aggression of others.

While women are treated as sexual objects our sexuality is defined by male society. We are expected not to enjoy sex. We are told it is our responsibility to control pre-marital relations and to serve our husbands sexual whims in marriage. Because we are expected to control the situation or to serve the needs of others we can never explore our own sexuality.

The cult of female virginity is a symbol of male control. It keeps the women in line by labeling those who dare to refuse to become slaves as loose women, whores, and concubines. It sets the rebels and the virgins against each other and guarantees continued control by men.

Sexuality in our society is intimately related to the roles assigned to men and women. The man is expected to be aggressive, strong, virile, self-centered, ... while the woman is expected to be self sacrificing, passive, docile, weak, and responsive to men's initiatives. These roles ensure the oppression of women by men in a heterosexual relationship. ...

The Woman as Domestic Slave: A married woman is expected to be the domestic slave of her husband (often it is even stated in the marriage ceremony: "the wife shall be subject to her husband"). It is her duty to cook his meals, wash his clothes, clean his house, and raise his kids. It goes without saying that she receives no salary for this work, except what he graciously decides to give her. She is expected to be subservient to him, to obey his request and orders. He gives her whatever liberties he chooses because he is 'king of his castle'.

BURCK IN THE CHICAGO SUN-TIMES

Declaration of Independence II

A REPLY TO WOMEN'S LIBERATION

by Mrs. Kathy Teague*

Mrs. Teague, the Executive Secretary of the Charles Edison Youth Fund, wrote the following article as a response to ''A Conservative View of Women's Liberation,'' which appeared in the April 1972 issue of **New Guard**. **New Guard** is a monthly published by Young Americans for Freedom, a conservative youth group.

Examine the following questions before beginning the reading:

1. What view of motherhood does Mrs. Teague feel is held by most families in our country?
2. What dangerous effect, according to Mrs. Teague, might the ''women's liberation'' movement have on our children?
3. What view does Mrs. Teague have of the slavery of women, as described in the previous reading? Do you agree?

*Kathy Teague, ''The Most Admired Women,'' **New Guard**, June, 1972, pp. 12-13. Reprinted with permission.

"She is the typical mother. She has devoted her days and often her nights to bestowing love and care on her children, and she has implanted in their minds and hearts love of God and of their neighbor. Without any expectation of material rewards or outside recognition she continues to meet the multitude of challenges presented to her each day. She knows in her own heart the special joys and rewards of being a mother. Even in the face of difficulties she completes her appointed tasks with faith in her offspring and unshaken confidence that she is doing God's will in the most natural, perfect vocation — motherhood. It is through her that the human and spiritual values essential for the betterment of the twentieth century are brought into the mainstream of modern life. And so, my admiration and esteem are extended to the mothers of today."

Those words of Mrs. Joseph P. Kennedy express a view of womanhood and motherhood that is shared and fostered in an overwhelming number of families in our country. Her simple words are a refreshing and welcome relief at a time when we are beseiged by the so-called "women's liberation" movement's unfounded, demeaning charges against women in general and motherhood in particular. ...

My own mother took pride in her role as a woman and wife and lovingly and unselfishly devoted many years of her life (the happiest, too, she tells me) to raising and educating her children. There was just never a question as to whether men were better than women or vice versa. My parents instilled the belief in me that every person should be considered on his or her individual merits, regardless of that person's sex. ...

I'm not alone in my feelings. ... I have not talked with one woman — single or married — friend, acquaintence, or business associate, who was raised believing that "nothing they accomplish will be worth anything compared to the accomplishments of men." ...

If the "women's liberation" movement is concerned about the future of women in our country and the world, its supporters had better give some consideration to the people who hold that future in the palms of their hands — our children — the future leaders of America and of the world.

How will the "women's liberation" movement affect our children? Well, imagine as a child hearing your mother say that she felt like a slave; that she was bored with having to care for you and your home; that your father was an unappreciative slave driver; that she was deprived because she

28

had to stay home to cook, clean, and wash for you? Wouldn't you feel guilty — almost like an unwanted child. ...

What women's liberation should be fostering is more good mothers, who believe that their role as a mother is indeed a unique one. No woman should be subjected to countless television talk shows, newspaper and magazine articles wherein she is described as only a housewife — and a slave to her children and husband at that. How often does one hear or read about a wife and mother who said she felt totally fulfilled and happy in the vocation she had chosen. Surely the silent majority of women are united in spirit only and their feelings are rarely aired publicly. If half the time and space given to women's liberation was devoted to thoughtful advice and guidance for women who want to become better wives and mothers, then all women would truly be taking a giant step forward.

The women's liberation movement does itself and all women a great disservice by demeaning the vocation of marriage and motherhood, which a woman freely chooses to enter. ... No woman is "sold into" marriage. And any woman who wants out can take advantage of the liberal divorce laws in this country. Moreover, as a result of our free enterprise system, which has produced the endless list of modern conveniences that make a woman's work far from drudgery, the American homemaker has more free time to devote to activities and interests outside her home than women anywhere else in the world.

The subject of homemaking and homekeeping brings me to another false generalization. ... ''But the fact is that men don't regard such a role (homemaking) as a praiseworthy lifetime occupation ... they have purposely dumped the whole game into our laps ... refusing to take on domestic tasks for fear of being reduced to the female level.'' Come on! All the husbands and fathers I know pitch in and help their wives take care of the children and the home. The husband who refuses to help his wife in the care of his family is surely the exception and not the rule.

No one is going to sell any woman the idea that being a homemaker is a glamorous job, but any well adjusted woman, who works hard to raise her family and make their home a happy and comfortable place to live, looks upon her day-to-day tasks of cooking and cleaning as a way of expressing her love. If a woman thinks that by leaving her family to fend for themselves and pursuing a career in the business and professional world she's going to find the ''ultimate'' satisfaction and a world free from boredom and routine — she is mistaken. All jobs have their routine tasks and all jobs haved their rewards. If she's bored at home, she's going to get bored at the office. A self-starter, always busy and engaged in something new and interesting, is going to be occupied and happy, whether she's in the office or at home.

ABILITY TO DISCRIMINATE

Usually difficult situations fail to present easy choices. Real life problems are too complex to permit simple choices between absolute right and wrong. The following exercise will test your ability to discriminate between degrees of truth and falsehood by completing the questionnaire. Circle the number on the continuum which most closely identifies your evaluation regarding each statement's degree of truth or falsehood.

1. Women have a more difficult role in our society than men.

   + — 5 4 3 2 1 0 1 2 3 4 5 —
   completely   partially   partially   completely
      true   true   false   false

2. The majority of American women are satisfied with the present system of inequality and special privilege they experience.

   + — 5 4 3 2 1 0 1 2 3 4 5 —
   completely   partially   partially   completely
      true   true   false   false

3. The primary interest the typical male has in women is one of sexual gratification.

   + — 5 4 3 2 1 0 1 2 3 4 5 —
   completely   partially   partially   completely
      true   true   false   false

4. When the male is the financial supporter of his family he should also be the ultimate authority in the household.

+ $\dfrac{\quad 5 \quad 4 \quad 3 \quad 2 \quad 1 \quad 0 \quad 1 \quad 2 \quad 3 \quad 4 \quad 5 \quad}{\text{completely} \qquad \text{partially} \qquad \text{partially} \qquad \text{completely}}$ −

completely   partially   partially   completely
  true   true   false   false

5. The women's liberation movement will probably harm our society more than help it.

+ $\dfrac{\quad 5 \quad 4 \quad 3 \quad 2 \quad 1 \quad 0 \quad 1 \quad 2 \quad 3 \quad 4 \quad 5 \quad}{}$ −

completely   partially   partially   completely
  true   true   false   false

6. Men and women should be completely equal before the law.

+ $\dfrac{\quad 5 \quad 4 \quad 3 \quad 2 \quad 1 \quad 0 \quad 1 \quad 2 \quad 3 \quad 4 \quad 5 \quad}{}$ −

completely   partially   partially   completely
  true   true   false   false

7. The inferior status of women in our society has a cultural basis rather than a biological one.

+ $\dfrac{\quad 5 \quad 4 \quad 3 \quad 2 \quad 1 \quad 0 \quad 1 \quad 2 \quad 3 \quad 4 \quad 5 \quad}{}$ −

completely   partially   partially   completely
  true   true   false   false

THE OPPRESSION
OF THE FEMALE SEX

by Mrs. Daisy K. Shaw*

Daisy K. Shaw is the Director of Educational and Vocational Guidance of New York City, and past president, Directors of Guidance of Large City School Systems of the American Personnel and Guidance Association. Her remarks below were originally delivered before the Special Subcommittee on Education and Labor of the U.S. House of Representatives.

The following questions should help your understanding of the reading:
1. What does Mrs. Shaw feel are the causes of the underrepresentation of women in the professions and prestigious positions?
2. What point is the author making when claiming that girls are constantly reminded of the need to be attractive?
3. Why is there a concentration of women in clerical occupations, teaching, nursing, sales and service occupations?

*From testimony introduced into the **Congressional Record** by Congresswoman Shirley Chisholm on March 9, 1971.

Although women represent a majority of 51 percent of our population, they suffer from many of the same barriers to economic and social progress as do minority groups in our society. They are paid less than men for comparable work, are often consigned to menial or routine jobs, are passed over for promotion, have a higher unemployment rate than men, and are grossly underrepresented in decisionmaking posts in politics, business, and the professions. These facts are well documented in numerous reports published by the Department of Labor, the Department of Commerce, the Women's Bureau, and various commissions and task forces.

Now, as never before, discrimination against women calls for strong new legislative action as well as vigorous enforcement of existing statutes. However, legislative remedies alone are not enough. What is needed is a thoroughgoing reappraisal of the education and guidance of our youth to determine what factors in our own methods of child rearing and schooling are contributing to this tragic and senseless underutilization of American women. For, as long as women perceive themselves as inferior, and as long as men cast them in subservient roles, legislation alone, though helpful, will not produce any substantive change in the status of American women. Fifty years after women's suffrage was won in the United States, we find only one woman in the Senate and 10 women in the House of Representatives. At the risk of being accused of female chauvinism, may I add that their quality is very high.

How do perceptions of sex roles develop? There is an old popular song of the forties that starts: "You have to be taught before it's too late, before you are six or seven or eight***." From their earliest years, children are introduced to picture books which practically condition them to accept males as the commanding, dominant figures in their lives. In a fascinating article published recently in the children's section of the New York Times book review, Elizabeth Fisher found that there were five times as many males in the titles of picture books as females, and that even animals in books are male for the most part. Furthermore, says Miss Fisher, even when females are depicted, their activities are quite limited.

They do not drive cars. Though children see their mothers driving all the time, not a single description or picture of a woman driver could I find. In the world today, women are executives, stockbrokers, taxi-drivers, steelworkers; in picture books these are nonexistent — though there have been women doctors in this country for over a hundred years, and pediatrics is one of their preferred specialties, there is not a single woman doctor to be found. Women are nurses, librarians, teachers — but the principal is always male. ...

Let us move from the preschool years to the kindergarten. Here little girls are still encouraged to "play house" in the homemaking corner, while little boys are building, firefighting, or policing. If one examines the primers used in the first three grades of elementary school, one searches in vain for a woman depicted as a worker (except for the omnipresent teacher and an occasional nurse, waitress, or secretary). Even the most up-to-date basic readers, issued in endless series by the leading publishers, are still presenting Dick and Jane types having endless fun, while mommy waits innocuously at the garden gate or in the apartment to welcome daddy home from a hard day at the office. (By contrast, the wicked queens of the old fairy tales at least displayed some executive talent.) It is true that there has been an effort during the past few years on the part of some publishers to update reading material used in the elementary schools. However, these changes have been largely confined to presenting a more balanced view of ethnic diversity in the urban environment. With a few outstanding exceptions, as in the Bank Street readers, women are still being portrayed in the same old stereotyped roles. ...

These subtle concepts, imprinted on children's minds in the early school years, are reinforced during adolescence by the communications media. Girls are constantly reminded of the need to be attractive, so that they can acquire a mate who will provide them with all the material comforts. Labor-

THE PURPOSE OF WOMEN IS TO PLEASE MEN

The whole education of women ought to be relative to men. To please them, to be useful to them, to make themselves loved and honored by them, to educate them when young, to care for them when grown, to counsel them, to console them, and to make life sweet and agreeable to them — these are the duties of women at all times and what should be taught them from their infancy.

Jean Jacques Rosseau

saving devices are advertised as easing the lot of the house-wife, rather than that of the working woman — or man, for that matter. Plenty of men use laundromats, but you never see one proclaiming that his wash is "brighter than bright." With the constant and prolonged emphasis on the need to please rather than the need to be someone, it is small wonder that many girls choose easier or less time-consuming courses of study than boys, and frequently give more attention to the social rather than the intellectual aspects of college life.

The sex label would seem to be a cultural rather than a biological factor in the labor market. The concentration of women in clerical occupations, teaching, nursing, sales, and service occupations is based on cultural factors and societal expectations rather than on sex-linked characteristics or aptitudes. ...

While training for a career continues to play a central role in the education of boys, the importance of career planning for girls is less clearly understood. As the role expectations of American women continue to change in this era of techno-logical progress and automation, counselors are faced with an important question: "Should counseling be different for girls than for boys?" ...

The "self-image" of the individual girl is strongly in-fluenced by society's expectation of her role. Although labor market analysts estimate that 9 out of every 10 girls in school today become workers at some time in their lives, many are still indoctrinated with the idea that work will be an optional, incidental part of their lives, if indeed they will ever work at all. Some believe a Prince Charming will carry them off and they will live happily forever after.

WOMEN HELP OPPRESS THEMSELVES

by Thyra Thomson*

Thyra Thomson was elected Wyoming's first woman secretary of state in 1962 and reelected in 1966 and 1970.

Use the following questions to help your understanding of the reading:
1. How do women help oppress themselves, in the opinion of Thyra Thomson?
2. Why does the author believe that the women's liberation movement will help men more than women?

*From "Who Needs Women's Lib?" by Thyra Thomson, **Denver Post**, February 21, 1971. Reprinted with permission from the **Denver Post** and Thyra Thomson.

Every time I read about Women's Lib demonstrators burning their bras or crashing for-men-only saloons, I wonder when the voice of sweet reason will penetrate the current crusade for women's rights.

I think it's time women admitted we've had equal rights a long time. We simply haven't done much with them. ...

Most women don't worry about equality with men when they are young. They're too wrapped up in the primeval desire to love and be loved, to marry and to nest. I doubt if many young women think beyond the day when they don a wedding veil.

Yet it is a fact of modern life that 8 out of 10 women work outside the home, and 64 percent of the women who work are married. And those who return to work after having a family can expect to spend 23 years on the job.

How galling it is, when a woman does return to work, to realize she is locked into the lower-paid, tedious jobs. She will not only probably make less money than a man, but have far less chance of promotion.

Yet I must point out that there is no law confining women to inferior jobs. Women themselves must bear a large share of the blame for their plight. Women don't buck for promotion the way men do. Men look forward to a better job, and expect it. Women don't. They can handle responsibility as well as men, but too many women seem to think it's unfeminine to do so.

The underlying problem is that women are not motivated by job prestige. A man may be measured by his work, but a woman measures herself by her success with men. That's something Women's Lib wants to change, and if this means judging women as people rather than sex objects, I'm all for it. But I wouldn't want to change the innate desire of women to be attractive to men.

Instead, I'd like to teach them that for many years of their lives, they have to be attractive to employers, too. Let's teach women how to get a job as well as how to get a man. And let's teach them early.

Most women don't really plan careers until they're "empty nesters" in their 30s. Unless a woman prepares for that work before marriage, while she's still in school, she may not find her career opportunities satisfying, useful or equal. ...

I wish we could see equality as something we share "with" men instead of trying to be the "same as" men.

Still, I have a hunch the men won't suffer. In fact, I believe that in the long run the Women's Lib movement will help men more than it does women.

Women will eventually achieve wage parity: equal pay for equal work. When they do, employers will probably hire more men, and more women will stay home.

An indirect result of men's demanding higher and higher pay in the past was that women were hired. It was simple economics. Women worked for less.

When men and women command identical pay, women will forfeit the advantage of being low bidders and probably will end up with fewer jobs.

Women have some disadvantages in job hunting. While the empty-nester going back to work becomes a faithful, stable employee, her skills are usually rusty and her education out of date. She starts again at the bottom of the ladder and pay scale.

Young women on the other hand usually don't stay on the job long enough to warrant training them for well paid, responsible positions.

They average less than two years. Marriage, or a baby, or a husband being transferred are the major reasons they quit. And they don't see anything wrong with that. ...

Men are far more willing to do the extra-curricular chores that lead to the top. They volunteer for Chamber of Commerce work, serve on committees — all the extra things that are part of the climb to management positions. Most women put that extra time into their families.

I don't know whether it's simply custom, or deep-seated instinctive urges that cause women to do this, but the point I want to make is that women ought to do what makes them happy. And they shouldn't blame men if they aren't happy at what they're doing.

For most women, true happiness is in helping the men in their lives to their mutual goals. They are working with their mates, and I can't think of a more noble objective in life. ...

We can't blame men alone for inequalities that still exist. We have to liberate ourselves by changing our attitudes and accepting the reality of a world which requires us to be both wives and workers.

Somehow I find it difficult to view men as the enemy.

ABILITY TO EMPATHIZE

The ability to empathize, to see life and its problems through another person's eyes, is a skill you must develop if you intend to learn from the experiences of others.

Consider the following true life situation:

An American school teacher underwent a sex change operation from male to female. This individual, Mr. Smith for discussion purposes, is now known as Mrs. Smith. She continues to live with her wife and three children.

Mrs. Smith teaches elementary school and has experienced pressure from the school board to transfer from elementary school to high school within the school district. The school board has also asked Mrs. Smith to resign and obtain a new teaching certificate in her female name. Mrs. Smith has refused, and because of the refusal the board has asked the state board of education to remove her tenure.

What personal and public complications do you see in this situation?

(Try to imagine how the following individuals would react to this situation. What reasons do you think they would give for their actions?)

> The district school board chairman
> A student spokesman for Mrs. Smith
> A mother in favor of Mrs. Smith's firing
> Mrs. Smith
> A practicing Christian
> Mrs. Smith's wife
> Mrs. Smith's oldest child
> You

PREMARITAL SEX: SHOULD YOU OR SHOULDN'T YOU?

THE CASE FOR PREMARITAL SEX

by Albert Ellis*

Dr. Ellis is currently the Executive Director of the Institute for Advanced Study in Rational Psychotherapy. He has practiced psychotherapy and family counseling for over 25 years in New York City. Some of his best known books are **Sex Without Guilt, A Guide to Rational Living, Homosexuality: Its Causes and Cure** and **How to Prevent Your Child from Becoming A Neurotic Adult.**

As you read consider the following questions:
1. Dr. Ellis lists the advantages of premarital sex relations. Which do you think make the most sense?
2. Are there other advantages to premarital sex that Ellis fails to mention?

*Albert Ellis, **Sex Without Guilt** (Lancer Books, Inc., 1966), pp. 46-51. Reprinted with permission from the publisher and the author.

There are ... many obvious benefits to be derived from antenuptial sex relations. Here are some of them:

1. Sexual release. Most human beings require some form of steady sexual release for their maximum healthfulness, happiness, and efficient functioning. If these individuals are not married — which many millions of them, of course, are not — perhaps the best form of relief from sexual tension they may obtain is through having heterosexual premarital relations.

2. Psychological release. In many, though by no means all instances, individuals who do not have premarital affairs are beset with serious psychosexual strain and conflict and tend to be obsessed with sexual thoughts and feelings. Most of these individuals can be considerably relieved of their psychosexual hypertension if they have satisfactory non-marital affairs.

3. Sexual competence. In sexual areas, as in most other fields of human endeavor, practice makes perfect and familiarity breeds contempt for fear. In the cases of millions of unmarried males and females who are relatively impotent or frigid, there is little doubt that if they engaged in steady heterosexual relations they would become enormously more sexually competent.

4. Ego enhancement. Although ... engaging in premarital affairs involves distinct risks, especially the risks of being rejected or emotionally hurt, there is almost no other way that a human being can enhance his self-esteem and desensitize himself to emotional vulnerability except by deliberately taking such risks.

Confirmed male and female virgins in our culture usually dislike themselves immensely, knowing that they do not have the guts to live.

5. Adventure and experience. A rigorous restraint from premarital affairs leads to neutrality or nothingness: to a lack of adventure and experience. Particularly in this day and age, when there are few remaining frontiers to explore and unscaled mountains to climb, nonmarital affairs furnish a prime source of sensory-esthetic-emotional experimentation and learning.

6. Improved marital selection. Because marriage, in our society, is usually infrequent and long-lasting for any given individual, the person who marries should have the kind of knowledge and training that will best fit him to make a good marital choice. There is little doubt that the very best experience he can acquire in this connection is to have one or more premarital affairs and, through these affairs, be able to discover much relevant information about himself and members of the other sex. ...

7. Prophylaxis against sexual deviation. As will be pointed out elsewhere in this book, many individuals in our society become involved in fixed or exclusive homosexuality, or in other forms of sex fetishism or perversion, largely because they do not have ample opportunity for early heterosexual involvements. Premarital relations doubtless constitute the best possible prophylaxis to the development of serious psychosexual deviations.

8. Heterosexual democratization. The maintenance of premarital virginity, particularly among females, most inevitably leads to a double standard of sex morality and to fascistic-type discrimination against equal rights for women. Widespread premarital affairs invariably break down this autocratic, anti-female attitude and lead to real democracy and equality between the sexes.

9. Decrease in jealousy. Violent jealousy between men and women is largely the result of the banning of extramarital affairs and the viewing of one's mate as one's exclusive property. This kind of pathological jealousy would probably tend to be distinctly reduced if a more liberal attitude toward premarital affairs were extant.

10. De-emphasis on pornography. The increasing emphasis on the female form and on pornographic presentations that is currently so widespread in our culture is largely fomented by our restrictions on premarital sexuality. The more an individual engages in satisfactory and consistent premarital relations, the less he will usually be inclined to be interested in second-hand picturizations of sex. ...

11. Savings in time and energy. Considerable time is wasted in our society by individuals constantly seeking for direct or indirect sex gratifications in the path of which we place unusual obstacles. Those persons who actually engage in steady premarital affairs save this kind of wasted effort and at least considerably enjoy the time that they do devote to sexual participations.

12. Ending of sex discrimination. Many individuals in our culture for one reason or another do not care to marry or are in no position to do so for the present. There is no reason why these individuals should be discriminated against sexually merely because they are nonmaritally inclined.

By permitting these individuals to have premarital affairs, antisexual discriminations against them would thereby be removed. As things stand, however, many such individuals, who really should not marry or procreate, are literally driven into unhappy matings because they require sex outlets.

13. Sexual varietism. Many individuals have distinct needs for sexual varietism, especially during certain periods of their lives. The most practical way for these persons to fulfill their needs is through premarital affairs.

14. Limiting prostitution. There is no question that wherever premarital sex relations on a voluntary basis become more common, prostitutional relations tend to decrease considerably. If prostitution is thought to have distinct dangers and hazards, then the best way to eradicate these would be to encourage premarital non-prostitutional affairs.

15. Limiting abortion, illegitimacy, and venereal disease. If the facts of premarital relations were squarely faced and provided for, it would be a relatively simple matter to minimize or eradicate the danger of abortion, illegitimacy, and venereal disease. It is by combating premarital affairs that we fruitlessly employ efforts that could be much better spent in eliminating certain dangers which, almost entirely because of puritan bolstering, are still connected with such affairs.

16. Inhibiting sex offenses. Most sex offenders, as demonstrated in the book, **The Psychology of Sex Offenders** (Ellis and Brancale, 1956), are not overly impulsive, promiscuous individuals with wide-spread experience; on the contrary, they are overly-inhibited constricted persons with relatively little heterosexual experience. If these individuals would engage in more frequent, more satisfying premarital affairs, there is little doubt that many of them would commit fewer sex offenses.

17. Sex is fun. As has been previously noted by myself and others, sex is fun; heterosexual relations, in particular, are the very best fun; and more heterosexual relations are still more fun.

Assuming that human beings who remain virginal till marriage are more pure and saintly than those who do not, the thesis cannot very well be upheld that they are commonly happier and more joyful. To fornicate may be "sinful"; but it is also a rare delight. Perhaps we would be saner to work at making it less rare than less delightful.

SEXUAL FREEDOM LEAGUE STATEMENT

The Sexual Freedom League believes that sexual expression, in whatever form agreed upon between consenting persons of either sex, should be considered an inalienable human right. Sex without guilt and restriction is good, pleasurable, relaxing, and promotes a spirit of human closeness, compassion and good will. We believe that sexual activity has a wealth of potential for making life more livable and enjoyable.

The Sexual Freedom League exists to change repressive laws and puritan attitudes, and is working toward a free society.

Sexual Freedom League
P.O. Box 1276
Berkeley, California 94701

THE CASE FOR PREMARITAL CHASTITY

by Evelyn Millis Duvall*

Dr. Duvall is known nationally and internationally as a topranking authority on sex and family life education. Complementing her lectures and personal appearances here and abroad are her many articles, best selling books and widely adopted high school and college textbooks. She is an honorary life member of the National Council on Family Relations and a former executive in that organization.

Reflect on the following questions while you read:

1. Dr. Duvall points out several disadvantages to premarital sex. Which do you think make the most sense?
2. Are there other disadvantages to premarital sex that Duvall fails to mention?

*Evelyn Millis Duvall, **Why Wait Till Marriage?** (Association Press, 1965), pp. 32-38. Reprinted with permission from Association Press.

Premarital sex experience is often anything but enjoyable. There are several reasons why going all the way before marriage frequently brings more pain than pleasure.

1. First sex experiences are often disappointing. The fellow becomes too excited too quickly. He may appear impotent or unable to sustain an erection long enough at first. It takes time for a girl to awaken sexually before she, too, can respond. She must become gradually accustomed to sexual activity before she finds it even comfortable. The physical act between two partners who move at different tempos is frequently unpleasant. The married couple develop their own harmony as they each learn and teach one another the language of love, in time. But such "music" is rare at first. ...

2. Adequacy as male and female is hard to establish in premarital sex experience. Dr. Flanders Dunbar reminds us that teenagers know that a rule is being broken when they go all the way before marriage. This fact interferes with their communication as partners. Because each feels a little anxious and a little guilty, the girl is likely to be frigid and the boy at least partially impotent. They may be left with the feeling that they are inadequate human beings when the very thing they set out to prove was their competence. ...

3. Sex alone is not a strong bond. It is widely recognized that some fellows are active sexually with "bad" girls even while they are going with "good" girls. While they respect their sweethearts and are willing to wait for marriage before insisting upon sex experience with them, they relieve their sex drives with the kind of girl they would not consider marrying. Pick-ups are not hard to find. ...

These contacts are momentary and transitory. The promiscuous girl has no hold on the men with whom she consorts. They are literally here tonight and gone tomorrow. There is no bond of loyalty or sense of unity in this kind of sex experience. If there are personal feelings at all, they are likely to be of revulsion and relief once the physical act is over.

An impersonal attitude toward sex partners is common. Dr. Kinsey found that an overwhelming tendency of sexually promiscuous women was to feel callous and complacent about their behavior. They have more sex affairs before and after they marry. But they find less meaning in them. It is the familiar refrain of having more but enjoying it less. ...

4. Personal communication is central in sexual fulfillment. The better the couple know each other, and the communication they have before their sex experience, the more emotionally meaningful it is. ...

It takes time for a boy and girl to get through to one another as persons. If they rush into sexual activity, they run the risk of cutting off their chances of getting to know and love one another as persons. When that happens, even their sex life lacks the possibility of fulfillment, because it is not founded upon personal communication. ...

5. Guilt is a real possibility. There are couples who report that they have no feelings of guilt at having sex experience before marriage. ...

There is no doubt that other people suffer serious guilt feelings from having gone all the way before marriage. They feel guilty that they have not done the right thing. They are torn within themselves for having gone beyond their own standards. Guilt, recriminations, and blame often go together. One young woman says, for instance:

> I came back to reality with a sickening thud. I wasn't drunk any more. Nothing was funny now. The party was over and I felt sick, cheap, and dirty. It didn't make me feel any better to hear him say, "Why on earth didn't you stop us before things went too far? You should have known what would happen. You could have called a halt any time. But you didn't."

Guilt feelings are most frequent among those with high moral standards. Young people who have grown up in good homes are apt to feel guilty when they do something they have been taught is wrong. ...

6. Fear of discovery keeps many an unmarried couple from full enjoyment of their intimacy. Because it is generally considered wrong, the boy and girl approach each other with anxiety. Their ears are alert for any possible witness to their indiscretion. Their attention cannot be entirely upon each other, so long as they are afraid of being caught. Even if what they are doing has gone undetected so far, there is always the danger that somehow someone will find out. ...

7. The need for concealment of premarital sexual intercourse gives little or no security to the relationship. The couple has to sneak off in ways designed to deceive. The clandestine contact has to be stealthy to come off at all. The pair plot their coming together in some secret time and place that they hope will escape notice. They watch for moments when their intimacy will have at least some semblance of privacy, even in a public setting.

The thrill of forbidden fruit is like a small boy's enjoyment of stolen apples. More mature couples find that the stealthy quality of their contact makes them feel cheap. The relationship of even the most devoted pair seems shabby when it must be shrouded in secrecy. Lovers usually want to tell the world how they feel. But this is rarely possible in premarital affairs.

8. Haste is a risk for many an unmarried couple. Pleasure in sexual intimacy requires a sense of leisure all too often lacking before marriage. A man and wife can look forward to long, quiet evenings together.They can take all the time for the mutual loving and being loved that bring fulfillment to them both. They can prepare for their coming together with all the pleasant accompaniments that make their relationship throb with significance. Soft music, their favorite scents, special arrangements that heighten their pleasure in each other can be arranged in advance. Their lovemaking is in their own bed, admidst surroundings that they have lovingly prepared. A married couple's sex life can be richly varied and full of ritual because they have time to develop a repertoire of response to one another.

The young pair before marriage all too often have to snatch what they can get where they can get it. Their contact is suffused with urgency. The girl, and often the boy, too, is left unsatisfied even after having gone through the motions of going all the way.

9. Being exploited is no fun. One of the disillusioning aspects of premarital sex for the girl is feeling that she simply has been used for the boy's pleasure. ...

10. Uneven commitment is not funny. One of the differences between the sexes is that sexual relations tend to make the female more possessive of her man. She tends to become more emotionally involved with her sex partner than he does with her. Once premarital sex is underway, the girl urges permanence and "getting things settled". But it is when she becomes too demanding that he is most likely to want to regain his freedom. ...

The unpleasant side effects of premarital sexual relations are not funny to either the girl or the fellow. Doctors report that such symptoms as depression, ennui, inability to study, to sleep, or to eat often accompany the turmoil of uneasy love. It piles up so heavily that the relationship between two compatible sweethearts can break under the strain. This is one reason why so many devoted couples break their engagements rather than go on into marriage. They did not know the effect their intimacy would have on their relationship until it was too late. They get in too deep, too fast, and then cannot go through with their plans. They separate, and each tries to put the pieces of life together.

A CASE STUDY

This case study examines the sexual practices of two very different cultures, one in Ireland and the other in the South Pacific. Although these cases represent extremes, they can be helpful in causing you to evaluate the sexual customs of our country, as well as those of your community and peer group.

The Lack of the Irish?
  by John C. Messenger

Too Much in Mangaia?
  by Donald S. Marshall

*Excerpted from Chapter 1, "Sex and Repression in An Irish Folk Community" by John C. Messenger and Chapter 5, "Sexual Behavior on Mangaia" by Donald S. Marshall, in **HUMAN SEXUAL BEHAVIOR**, edited by Donald S. Marshall and Robert Suggs. © 1971 by the Institute for Sex Research, Inc., Basic Books, Inc., Publishers, New York.

THE LACK OF THE IRISH?

Misconceptions about sex and lack of sexual knowledge among adults make Ireland's Inis Beag one of the most sexually naive of the world's societies, past or present. Sex is never discussed in the home when children are about; almost no mothers advise their daughters. Boys are better advised than girls, but the former learn about sex informally from older boys and men as well as from what they see animals do. Adults rarely give sexual instruction to youths, believing that after marriage nature takes its course, thus negating the need for anxiety-creating and embarrassing personal confrontations between parents and their offspring. ...

Sexual misconceptions are myriad in Inis Beag. The islanders share with most Western peoples the belief that men by nature are far more sexually disposed than women. Women are taught by the curate and in their home that sexual relations with their husbands are a duty that must be ''endured,'' for to refuse coitus is a mortal sin. A frequently encountered Inis Beag assertion affixes the guilt for male libidinal strivings on their enormous intake of potatoes. Asked to compare sexual proclivities of Inis Beag men and women, one woman said, ''Men can wait a long time before wanting 'it,' but we can wait a lot longer.'' ...

Inis Beag men share the belief, common in many primitive and folk societies, that sexual intercourse is debilitating. They will desist from sex the night before they are to do a job that takes great energy. They do not approach women sexually during menstruation or for months after childbirth; a woman is considered dangerous to the male at these times. ...

Nudity. Many kinds of behavior that other societies disassociate from sex — nudity, for example, and evacuation of bowel and bladder — are considered sexual in Inis Beag. Islanders abhor nudity. The consequences of this attitude are numerous and significant for health and survival. Only an infant has his entire body sponged on Saturday nights; children, adolescents and adults on the same night wash only their faces, necks, lower arms, hands, lower legs and feet. ...

Clothing is always changed in private, sometimes under the bedcovers, and islanders ordinarily sleep in their underclothes. ...

Parents and relatives severely punish any direct or indirect sexual expression by children — masturbation, mutual exploration of bodies, use of either standard or slang words relating to sex and open urination and defecation. Mothers take care to cover the bodies of infants in the presence of their siblings and outsiders, and sex is never discussed before children.

TOO MUCH IN MANGAIA?

Sex — sex for pleasure and sex for procreation — is a principal concern of the Polynesian people on tiny Mangaia, the southernmost of the Cook Islands near the geographical center of Polynesia in the South Pacific. From early puberty, Mangaians of both sexes reflect this concern in the numerous words they have for coitus, for the sexual parts and for sexual activities, and in the language of their insults. ...

There is great directness about sex, but the approach to sex is correspondingly indirect. Among the young there is no dating, no tentative necking in the American sense. A flick of the eye, a raised eyebrow in a crowd, can lead to copulation — without a word. There is no social contact between the sexes, no rendezvous, that does not lead directly to coitus — copulation is the only imaginable outcome of heterosexual contact. The sexual intimacy of copulation precedes personal affection. ...

Mangaian parents encourage their daughter to have sexual experiences with several men. They want her to find the man who is the most congenial — among those whose other social and material assets make them eligible. But they do not really want her to be pregnant until she finds the right man. Mangaians believe that it is continued coitus with the same man that causes pregnancy.

"Bull." Traditionally, a male goes from female to female — leaving one when he tires or wants variety or hears that she has gone with another man. Mangaians admire the boy who has had many girls: "A strong man, like a bull, going from woman to woman." ...

Deviance. There is no trace of active homosexuality in either sex on Mangaia, where very nearly everything is known about very nearly everybody. ...

Bastardy does not carry the social stigma in Mangaia that it does in the Western world, although the encroachment of Western law and custom now is beginning to place the illegitimate individual at a social and financial disadvantage. Because of complex kinship and incest prohibitions a couple may have three or more children, yet still may be refused parental permission to marry and to live together formally. ...

Magaians assert that husband and wife come together only to copulate. ...

Certainly one observes no telling of casual stories or small talk, no public displays of affection, no calling of pet names, no hand-holding. Even money is handled separately by husbands and wives; their trading-store charge accounts are kept separate. But affection does seem to come to married partners with age.

BIAS AND REASON

One of the most important critical thinking skills is the ability to distinguish between opinions based on emotions or bias and conclusions based on a rational consideration of facts. This discussion exercise is designed to promote experimentation with one's capacity to recognize biased statements.

Some of the following statements have been taken from the first eleven readings and some have other origins. Consider each statement carefully. Mark (R) for any statement you feel is based on a rational consideration of the facts. Mark (P) for any statement you believe is based on prejudice or emotion. Mark (I) for any statement you think is impossible to judge. Then discuss and compare your judgments with other class members.

> R = REASON
> P = PREJUDICE
> I = IMPOSSIBLE TO JUDGE

_____1.　The family has withstood many attacks over the past centuries and will survive all present and future attacks.

_____2.　The nuclear family must be replaced with a new form of family that will meet more adequately the needs of all its members.

_____3.　Professional parents could do a better job of raising children than natural parents.

_____4.　The family is the best possible method of reproducing members of the race.

_____ 5. Children in a cluster group family would be better adjusted individuals than children in a traditional nuclear family.

_____ 6. The average woman works harder than the average man in our society.

_____ 7. The enslavement of women by men was the first form of oppression to appear in human history.

_____ 8. The husband who refuses to help his wife in the care of his family is surely the exception and not the rule.

_____ 9. Men are more industrious workers than women.

_____10. Most people who do not indulge in premarital sex relations are beset with serious psychosexual strain and conflict and tend to be obsessed with sexual thoughts and feelings.

_____11. Marriage is necessary if one is going to experience a satisfying long term sexual relationship with a member of the opposite sex.

_____12. Extra marital sex relations are always sinful.

_____13. The women's liberation movement has led to a great amount of homosexuality among women.

HOMOSEXUALS, DEVIATES OR JUST DIFFERENT?

Readings:

HOMOSEXUAL IS AN OPPRESSIVE TERM

by Jack Baker*

Jack Baker is studying law at the University of Minnesota and doing graduate work in business administration at Oklahoma City University. He received a Bachelor of Science Degree in industrial engineering from the University of Oklahoma. He has worked as an industrial engineer for E.I. du Pont de Nemours & Co., Inc., as an engineer for Dolese Bros. Co., and a contract administrator for the United States Air Force. He frequently appears as a guest lecturer on the problems and life style of Gay people and has  participated in radio and television programs dealing with homosexuality. In September, 1969 he was elected President of "FREE: Gay Liberation of Minnesota." In April, 1971 Jack Baker was elected President of the Minnesota Student Association for the University of Minnesota. In April, 1972 he became the first person to ever be reelected as President of the Minnesota Student Association for a second term.

*Jack Baker's reading was written at the editors' request for inclusion in this book.

What am I?

I have a bachelor of science degree in engineering, so I am a college graduate. I served in the Air Force, so I am a veteran. I have a masters degree in business administration and have worked in a corporation, so I am a business man. I go to law school, so I am a law student. Twice, I have been elected president of the largest student body in the country — the University of Minnesota — so I am a student leader.

But, I also live with another man. I have lived with him for over five years. I love him and we make love. Now what does that make me?

Many people would say then, that I am a "homosexual." But the word "homosexual" does not describe what I am. It does not tell you about my school work or my activities as a student leader. It does not tell you about the dreams that Mike and I have, or the tender moments we share eating dinner late at night. ...

The word "homosexual" is used to perpetuate the social myth that American citizens who love members of the same sex are "perverts" who hang around public bathrooms. At best, the word "homosexual" makes the reader think of sexual acts rather than love or dreams, or warm interpersonal relationships.

I am thirty years young. I have never had sex in a public bathroom. But you may have difficulty believing that because the word "homosexual" is attached to my name. I am very much in love with Mike. And I have been in love with him since I was twenty-five.

Yet you may not believe that either, because the word "homosexual" doesn't encourage images of Mike and me being happy.

For too long the word has implied only negative aspects of same-sex relationships. And so, when people hear the word "homosexual" attached to my name, they forget that I have three degrees and am a student leader. And they can't imagine that I get up early in the morning, shave with Michael, ride my bike to school, go to classes and committee meetings; that I come home to our modest apartment, that Mike and I kiss, that we eat dinner and study until ten, and then go to bed — together.

No. The word "homosexual" will never mean that. And as long as you can think of me as a "homosexual" you will never be able to think of me as a perfectly average person, who happens to be in love with another man. ...

Instead of communicating the idea of a warm relationship with a person of the same sex, the term "homosexual" evokes a picture of a person whose personality revolves around sexual gratification. It is precisely because the term communicates this inaccurate and misleading information that it is oppressive.

"Homosexual" stands for all the negativisms that the "heterosexual majority" would impose on us. It must be replaced with a term that implies an entire life style. Gay is such a term. It has come into current usage to remedy the negative ideas conveyed by the term "homosexual."

Contrary to the subtle innuendoes of the term "homosexual," Gay people are not pre-occupied with sex. Sexual activity is but a small part of a larger personality. It is an everyday occurrence to find Gay people interacting with persons for whom they have no sexual desire. The term Gay, then communicates a broad spectrum of interests.

Gay people are attempting to orient large metropolitan areas to their needs. Shops, theaters, restaurants are being designed with Gay people in mind. In this way, Gay people hope to build a sense of pride in their community. Gay, then means Gay pride.

In the years past, the political system did not respond to the needs of the Gay people. And in fact the different levels of government tried to punish Gay people for expression of same-sex love. Now, however, Gay people are uniting to make their demands heard, and their needs felt, at the ballot box. Gay then, is Gay Power.

To Gay people, Gay has a unique meaning — one that is conveyed through the experience of living. Gay to a Gay person is Black to a Black person. It communicates all the amenities of a same-sex life style — rejection of social roles, expressions of emotion towards persons of the same sex publicly, wearing of adornment, and the feeling of brotherhood or sisterhood.

The term "homosexual" must be rejected totally. In its place must be substituted the word Gay. Those who are not

Gay are nongay. And "homosexuality" must give way to a phrase that takes on an added dimension — "same-sex life style." Since oppression begins with terminology, then the terminology must be purified before an environment can be created that will accommodate social change.

Once you have been able to discard the old and misleading terminology, you will have made the first giant step toward truly understanding that Mike and I love each other — that we live in comfortable surroundings, with many friends, and that the only sad thing about our lives is that we are so busy studying and working in the community that we don't have enough time to be together.

HOMOSEXUALS ARE SICK

by Robert E. Gould, M.D.*

> Dr. Robert E. Gould is the Director of Adolescent Psychiatry at the Bellevue Medical Center in New York City. He is also an Associate Professor of Psychiatry at the New York University Medical Center.

The following questions should help you understand the reading:

1. How does Dr. Gould define the term homosexual?
2. According to the author what do most psychiatrists say about the emotional health of homosexuals?
3. Why does he think homosexuality can never be considered a normal way of life?

*Robert E. Gould, "Understanding Homosexuality," **Seventeen**, July, 1969, pp. 91, 128. Reprinted from **Seventeen** ® Copyright © 1969 by Triangle Publications, Inc. Reprinted with permission from the author.

The process by which someone becomes homosexually oriented is a complicated one. While it is true that occasional homosexual experiences in adolescence may fall into the "normal" range of behavior, they may also indicate abnormal tendencies that will lead the boy or girl into a homosexually-oriented style of life. There is no way to lump all homosexuals together as if they each had the same problem or personality. The only thing you know for sure about a homosexual is that he prefers as a sexual partner someone of his own sex, and that this represents both a deviation from the normal development and a problem in interpersonal relations. Most psychiatrists view homosexual behavior as a symptom of an emotional problem which varies, both in nature and in severity, from one individual to another.

The ways of expressing a personality disturbance are relatively limited, so that very different personality traits may produce similar kinds of behavior. A pattern of homosexuality per se does not tell you very much about how sick or healthy an individual is, what it means to him, and what if anything can and should be done about it. For example, a "homosexual" problem may be primarily not a sexual one at all, but rather a problem of dependency. Because of certain personal experiences, the expression of this dependency may become channeled into a homosexual outlet. ...

Although in any individual instance a girl may be "sicker" in her homosexuality than a boy, homosexuality in girls generally tends to be less severe and more amenable to treatment. There are a number of cultural reasons for this difference.

1. Women are permitted to express greater physical intimacy with each other than men are. Kissing and hugging are acceptable forms of friendly expression between girls, but not between boys (in our culture).

2. Two homosexual women may live together in complete intimacy in many communities without incurring social disapproval, so long as they do not flaunt their inversion (such as one partner's assuming very masculine dress or manners). Two men living together are subject to much hostility. This difference in attitude may be partly due to the biological fact that intimacy and close bodily contact can occur between women without overt evidence of sexual gratification; this is not true of two men in the same situation.

66

3. Men are still traditionally freer to seek women for sexual partnerships, although the difference is less today than it used to be. The double standard is fast disappearing. Nevertheless, an unattractive or old man still has less incentive to abandon a heterosexual course than does a woman with the same drawbacks. Even statistics (more women than men in the country) favor the man in the heterosexual sweepstakes.

4. Early heterosexual experimentation is more frowned on for girls than for boys.

5. Girls are often encouraged, seldom chastised for "tomboy" behavior. Boys evoke ridicule and disapproval for "sissy" behavior.

None of these cultural attitudes is in itself crucial or decisive, but when all are added together, they help explain why girls are more receptive to treatment for homosexual problems, and also why they are usually less rigidly set in their homosexual patterns than boys. In general, the more strongly an individual defies the cultural mores and social taboos, the stronger and more deeprcoted is his need to do so.

How can you tell when someone needs help with a homosexual problem? How should you feel about a friend or relative who may be developing homosexual preferences?

HOMOSEXUAL TRAITS

The late Dr. Edmund Bergler found certain traits present in all homosexuals, including inner depression and guilt, irrational jealousy and a megalomaniac conviction that homosexual trends are universal.

Time, January 21, 1966 describing the views on homosexuality of psychiatrist Edmund Bergler

One cannot avoid the question — usually argued most vocally, if not persuasively, by homosexuals themselves: can homosexuality ever be a normal way of life regarded simply as a matter of personal preference, like preferring steak to lobster, without any implication of neurosis?

67

Among psychiatrists, there is almost complete agreement that homosexuality represents a hidden emotional conflict (neurosis).

One would be more impressed with the homosexual's insistence that his sexual behavior merely represents personal choice if he ever had satisfactory heterosexual relationships and then said he preferred a homosexual way of life. I know of no psychiatrist (or anyone else) who has been able to document such an achievement.

One difference between a neurotic and a normal person is that the neurotic has only one way to do something even if that way is not too good. He has fewer options and less flexibility in situations that may require him to be adaptable. A neurotic (or homosexual) may function fairly well in a particular setting, whereas if he were subjected to different stresses, he might flounder badly.

Homosexuality, although a deviation in personality development, is neither more nor less sinister than many other disorders. Thus there is no reason for it to be singled out for any special stigma or disapproval, either on legal, social or religious grounds.

A MENTAL ILLNESS

I do not regard homosexuality as a mental illness. I regard it as a psychologically rooted sexual disorder in the same sense that I consider chronic frigidity in a woman or impotence in a man to be a neurotically evolved condition.

Psychiatrist Irving Bieber in "The Playboy Panel: Homosexuality," **Playboy**, April, 1971.

Words such as "degenerate" and other pejorative and derogatory epithets simply reflect the user's own ignorance, prejudice and perhaps his own unsolved problems in that very area. Psychiatrists well know that those who protest too much are in someway troubled themselves. If there is a latent homosexual problem which has not been "acted out," such a person may say: "If a homosexual ever approached me, I'd kill him." There is no rational reason for this overreaction except the urge for self-protection when one feels vulnerable.

Compassion and tolerance toward homosexuals are more rational reactions, and your ability to feel these emotions indicates that you are probably free of problems in this area.
...

Perhaps the most important reason for recognizing homosexual tendencies in adolescents is that so much more can be done for them than for adults, whose personalities and sexual identities are more definitely formed. Not only is the homosexual pattern less crystallized in the teenager, but often a therapist can change the destructive behavior patterns of his family. For the adult homosexual, this kind of help comes too late. Homosexuality is treatable but generally not as an isolated character disorder.

Few people come to a psychiatrist with homosexuality as the chief complaint. It is generally an adaptive response to an underlying conflict. It helps relieve anxieties even if it cripples people in other ways. The psychiatrist, therefore, does not attempt to treat the homosexuality, but concentrates instead on whatever problem the patient himself wants to clear up. In working toward a better integration and growth of personality, underlying conflicts are either resolved or reduced, which may eliminate the symptom of homosexuality.

In seeking help, what both parents and teen-agers must try to understand is that treatment of the homosexual symptom is secondary to the promotion of a better over-all functioning of the human being. Not every homosexual can be "cured" and many don't want to be. For some it would be too painful. Again this is no different from certain other neurotics who have learned to live with their problems — occasionally with relative comfort.

Some homosexuals may be helped to function better and live more happily even if they remain homosexual. (This does not mean a psychiatrist only helps a person adjust better to his homosexuality!) Some homosexuals never seek treatment at all. They may not be unhappy enough to feel they need it.

If one looks at sexual orientation, then heterosexuality does offer a greater potential than homosexuality for enjoyment in life. Still, this can hardly be the sole or even the main criterion for judging relative mental health. Some heterosexuals are much sicker than some homosexuals who happen to be "well-adjusted" in their homosexual context.

It is possible for a good homosexual "marriage" (again in relative terms) to be more constructive than a heterosexual marriage that functions very badly. Homosexuals may "hate women" (or be afraid of them) and manifest this by avoiding them. That does not make them sicker than a heterosexual who hates women (or is afraid of them) and expresses it by marrying and then making the women totally miserable.

Homosexuality is treatable — or untreatable — depending on the circumstances, which differ with every individual. Understanding him as a person, not as a homosexual, is not only more constructive, it is healthier — both for him and his worried parents or friends.

DISTINGUISHING BETWEEN STATEMENTS THAT ARE PROVABLE AND THOSE THAT ARE NOT

From various sources of information we are constantly confronted with statements and generalizations about social and moral problems. In order to think clearly about these problems, it is useful if one can make a basic distinction between statements for which evidence can be found, and other statements which cannot be verified because evidence is not available, or the issue is so controversial that it cannot be definitely proved. Students should constantly be aware that social studies texts and other information often contain statements of a controversial nature. The following exercise is designed to allow you to experiment with statements that are provable and those that are not.

In each of the following statements indicate whether you believe it is provable (P), too controversial to be proved to everyone's satisfaction (C), or unprovable because of the lack of evidence (U). Compare and discuss your results with your classmates.

P = PROVABLE
C = TOO CONTROVERSIAL
U = UNPROVABLE

_____ 1. Gay people are emotionally ill.

_____ 2. Man is born with a sex drive that is neither same-sex nor opposite-sex oriented and a person's social environment determines if one will have a preference for sexual release with members of the same sex, the opposite sex or both.

_____ 3. If we judged all heterosexuals by those who see psychiatrists, we could conclude that all nongay people are sick.

_____ 4. The weight of modern scientific opinion runs strongly counter to the notion that gay people are mentally or emotionally ill.

_____ 5. More heterosexuals than homosexuals in high government positions have been found guilty of selling highly classified information to foreign agents.

_____ 6. In the recent history of Europe and North America, only two gay people have been blackmailed into handing over secrets to an enemy nation.

_____ 7. Recent studies show that gay people are no more prone to commit anti-social acts, sex offenses and other crimes, than heterosexuals.

_____ 8. Any kind of sexual activity is proper if it does not do harm to others.

_____ 9. About 10% of American males are predominately homosexual and 37% of all American men have at least one overt homosexual experience at some time in their lives.

_____ 10. The law should permit same-sex marriages.

_____ 11. The law should permit gay couples to adopt children.

_____ 12. Job discrimination against gay people should not be practiced by government or private employers.

THE SICKNESS THEORY REFUTED

by Dr. Louis Crompton*

Dr. Louis Crompton was born in 1925. He has written **Shaw The Dramatist** and edited **Dickens: Great Expectations** and **Shaw: Arms and the Man**. He is now a professor at the University of Nebraska and has previously taught at the University of Toronto and the University of British Columbia.

Examine this reading with the following questions in mind:

1. How does Dr. Crompton claim the sickness theory has influenced the social status of homosexuals?
2. According to the author what do most psychiatrists and other scientific authorities say about the emotional health of homosexuals?
3. What weaknesses does he find in the arguments supporting the theory that homosexuals are emotionally ill?

*Louis Crompton, **Homosexuality and the Sickness Theory** (Albany Trust 32 Shaftesbury Avenue London W1, 1969), pp. 3-7. Copyright © Louis Crompton 1969. This pamphlet is part of the Albany Trust's Talking Point series and is reprinted with permission of the author and publisher.

The idea that homosexuality is a sickness, all but unheard of fifty years ago, is now the prevailing opinion of the American public. When the Columbia Broadcasting System conducted a poll in connection with a televised documentary in 1966, seventy per cent of those interviewed classified homosexuality as a sickness, compared with only ten per cent who called it a 'crime' and nine per cent who called it a 'sin'. ...

There is strong evidence, indeed, that a classification of homosexuality as a disease has had just the opposite effect to what might have been hoped for. Instead of the public becoming more tolerant of homosexuals as sick people deserving sympathy, they have become more fearful. Nor, on consideration, is this really surprising. The average man is much more afraid of illness than of sin, and is particularly fearful of mental illness, and above all of mental illness that may effect a person's sexual conduct. The severity of our new state sexual psychopath laws testifies to this.

It is not surprising then that the position of the homosexual in American society — at least as far as official sanctions are concerned — is substantially worse than when the sickness theory was first formulated. The increase in discrimination against the homosexual has come about, paradoxically, in an age that is constantly congratulating itself in its freedom from the prejudices of the Victorians and the Puritans. ...

The first thing to note is that the weight of modern scientific opinion — except for one very important group to be noted below — actually runs strongly counter to the sickness hypotheses. Freud himself did not accept it. Neither did Havelock Ellis or Kraft-Ebing. ... The reader will find well-known specialists in the fields of anthropology, biology, clinical and social psychology, psychiatry, and sociology, who after extensive research and reflection have opposed the view that homosexuality is a form of sickness. When to such names as Freud and Kraft-Ebing, one adds those of Frank Beach, Harry Benjamin, Evelyn Hooker, Alfred Kinsey, Robert Lindner, Judd Marmor, Wardell Pomeroy, Michael Schofield, Thomas Szasz, and Ernest van den Haag, as well as the Wolfenden Committee, the most distinguished government group ever to undertake a study of the subject, it is obvious, to say the least, that the sickness theory does not command the universal acceptance in the scientific world which many liberals assume it does.

"Sorry, Mr. DaVinci, we are not permitted to employ
homosexuals."

But if the array of authorities on the anti-sickness side is
so formidable, where does the pro-sickness view gain its
support? The answer is, from a group of neo-Freudian psychoanalysts who, rejecting Freud's own stand, have argued
that homosexual behavior is ipso facto morbid. Despite the
large number of strongly contrary views expressed by many
other practicing psychoanalysts, it is this small but

influential group which has caught the attention of the public and appealed most strongly to its imagination.

Undoubtedly the two writers of this coterie who have had the widest influence on journalists and the reading public have been Edmund Bergler and Irving Bieber. The egregious Dr. Bergler is the author of a lively and sometimes brilliant diatribe entitled **Homosexuality: Disease or way of Life?** Despite the question mark in the title there is no doubt about Dr. Bergler's point of view. According to him, all homosexuals are sick men who are irrational, jealous, narcissistic, supercilious, hypersensitive, malicious, flippant, megalomaniacal, infantile, parasitic, and masochistic, and are, in addition, engaged in a diabolical conspiracy to dress women unattractively. Moreover, Dr. Bergler points out that homosexuals are given to protesting when they feel society has not treated them fairly, a dastardly trait which earns them the opprobrious epithet of 'injustice collectors'.

Though Dr. Bergler has been generally given a short shrift by his psychoanalytical colleagues (and even by others holding the sickness theory), he cannot, unfortunately, be dismissed as an interesting, if slightly maniacal, polemicist. His influence on the lay public has been enormous, thanks to his eminent readability and to his native genius for self-advertisement. Conservative moralists who a decade ago might have quoted St. Paul now quote Dr. Bergler. Time magazine's editorial of January 21, 1966 — probably the most widely read essay on homosexuality ever published — was markedly Berglerite throughout, right to its conclusion, which warned readers that whatever pity they might have in their hearts for homosexuals they were nevertheless not to let this emotion becloud the realization that they were here face to face with a ''pernicious disease.'' This, despite the fact that if Dr. Bergler had written in so biased a fashion about any other minority group, say Negroes or Jews, he would have raised a storm of dissent.

> Some psychiatrists get $50 an hour having homosexuals come to them for treatment. They'd be hesitant to say that homosexuals didn't need their treatment at all.

A homosexual being interviewed by Murry Frymer in ''Profile: A Militant Gay,'' **St. Paul Sunday Pioneer Press**, August 15, 1971.

If Dr. Bergler is a man with a bias, Dr. Bieber and his associates are men with a dogma. According to the book in which this group has set forth its conclusions (**Homosexuality: A Psychoanalytical Study**), ''all (sic!) psychoanalytical.'' ... The book has ... statistical charts ... of the questionnaires given by the authors to the one hundred and six homosexuals who were their patients.

But though the Bieber group is fully aware of the danger that besets scientific investigators of seeing only what they want to see and ignoring other evidence, it does not escape this pitfall. To begin with, to treat men in therapy as typical of America's several million homosexuals is like treating the patients in a mental ward as a typical sample in studying the nation's mental health. Furthermore, the questionnaires utilized were filled out, not by the patients or by neutral observers, but by researchers who were presumably predisposed to look at the men's emotional life in the light of a particular theory. How far this group is prepared to press its dogma that all male homosexuality is due to the fear of women can be seen from the fact that they explain not only the homosexuality of the streets and bars on this ground, but also that of the prison and isolated army camp. Since most of the temporary adaptations to homosexuality men make in such places are not due to fear of women but to their absence, this is patently absurd. In their case histories the group repeatedly ascribes actions to anxiety or fear where another observer might see other causes at work. Nor does their theory that over-solicitous mothers and indifferent fathers 'cause' homosexuality carry conviction. A generation or so ago psychoanalysts were ascribing homosexuality to exactly the opposite causes — cold mothers and affectionate fathers. The present tendency to make doting mothers responsible for their sons' social nonconformity has become a fashionable cliche, like the ''degeneration of the central nervous system'' that was used to explain all aberrant behavior at the turn of the century.

Clearly, what Dr. Bieber and his co-authors should have done was to have sat down with representatives from the three dozen or so homophile organizations fighting for homosexual rights throughout the nation, and on a man-to-man basis (as opposed to a doctor-patient one) tried to determine what it was that has kept these cheerful, energetic, and responsible business men, ministers, lawyers, teachers, journalists, civil servants and labourers out of doctors' offices, and has given them sufficient courage and self-respect to challenge our outmoded penal code, police harassment and entrapment, and job discrimination.

The fact is, however, that one does not go to a group of practicing psychoanalysts for an objective account of homosexuality any more than one goes to a cigarette company for an impartial study of the effects of tobacco. Psychoanalysts sell cures. That is how they make their living. There is nothing dishonourable in this, nor is there any reason to suppose that, taken as a whole, psychiatrists are not unusually intelligent and sympathetic men, genuinely concerned to help the emotionally upset people who seek them out. Still, if a doctor provides treatment for 350 hours (the course recommended by Bieber) at a cost of between $5,000 and $10,000 for homosexuals on the basis of a favourite theory, it is patently obvious that when this same doctor turns to discuss his ideas in print he is not an objective research worker, but a man with a commitment. In such cases a doctor's professional self-respect is not going to let him bring in a negative verdict against the assumptions and procedures he has been using. This is asking too much of human nature. ... Academically, the question as to whether one race is superior to another is still an open one. But it is not an open question politically. In the eyes of most men of good will the theory of racial supremacy is politically dead, killed off by its most ardent champions. The sickness theory of homosexuality is just beginning to have widespread legislative and social results. At this stage it behooves scientists and laymen alike to take a sharp and critical look at it.

HOMOSEXUALITY IS NATURAL

A psychoanalyst says that we are destined to heterosexual union, and anything that deviates from this must by definition be sick. This is nonsense even in animal terms. Animal communities can tolerate quite a lot of homosexual relationships ... two male geese can form a bond that is exactly like the bond between males and females. They function as a male-female pair; and geese, as far as I can see, are a very successful species.

Anthropologist Robin Fox in "A Discussion: Are Homosexuals Sick?," **Time**, October 31, 1969.

THE REALITIES
OF LESBIANISM

by Del Martin and Phyllis Lyon*

Phyllis Lyon, and her partner Del Martin, have recently co-authored a book on the Lesbian in a changing world. Phyllis Lyon is one of the founders of the Daughters of Bilitis, an international Lesbian Society started during 1965 in San Francisco. She has served as vice-president of the Council on Religion and the Homosexual, and as assistant director of the National Sex and Drug Forum.

Use the following questions to help you understand the reading:

1. How do the authors define a Lesbian?
2. What do they say is the Lesbian Stereotype?
3. Try to identify the legal and social sanctions they claim confront Lesbians.
4. What do they say causes a woman to become a Lesbian?

*From *The New Women,* edited by Joanne Cooke and Charlotte Bunchweeks, copyright (c) 1970, by The Bobbs-Merrill Company, Inc., reprinted by permission of the publisher.

The Lesbian minority in America, which may run as high as ten million women, is probably the least understood of all minorities and the most downtrodden. She has two strikes on her from the start; she is a woman and she is a homosexual, a minority scorned by the vast majority of people in our country. If, in addition, she is a member of a racial minority, it is hard sometimes to understand how she survives.

A Lesbian is a woman who prefers another woman as a sexual partner; a woman who is drawn erotically to women rather than to men. This definition includes women who have never experienced overt sexual relations with a woman — the key word is "prefers." There is really no other valid way to define the Lesbian, for outside of the sexual area she is as different in her actions, dress, status and behavior as anyone else. Just as there is no typical heterosexual woman, neither is there any typical Lesbian.

However, there is a popular misconception, or stereotype, of the Lesbian. She is believed to embody all the worst masculine attributes of toughness, aggressiveness, lack of emotion, lack of sentiment, overemphasis on sex, lack of stability — the need and desire to dress as a man or, at least, as much like a man as possible.

At some time in her life the Lesbian may fit this sterotype — usually when she is very young and just finding out about herself. After all, the Lesbian is a product of her heterosexual environment and all she has to go on, at her first awareness of Lesbian feeling in herself, is society's image. Part of the reason for her over-masculinization is the sexual identity of being attracted to women. At this point the Lesbian feels that in order to be attractive to another woman she must appear masculine. Another reason is for identification purposes. How will she meet other Lesbians? How will they know her to be one of them unless she indicates herself in an outward appearance? A third reason is one of releasing her hostility against society, of defying the mores which she finds stifling to what she considers her very being. A fourth reason is comfort. Any woman who says that girdles and high heels are comfortable is lying.

While it is true that occasionally a Lesbian gets trapped in this way of life (emulation of the male) and never finds her way to being a person rather than a symbol, the vast majority pass through this phase and learn to accept their femininity. As a Lesbian she comes to realize she is a human being first, a woman second, and a Lesbian only third. Un-

80

fortunately, however, society places the emphasis on the third — sexual identification — and does not acknowledge the Lesbian as a woman or a person.

But the average Lesbian (if there can be anything approaching "average" in our very complex world) is indistinguishable from other women in dress, in manner, in goals and desires, in actions and in interests. The difference lies in that she looks to women for her emotional and sexual fulfillment. She is a member of the family — a distant cousin, or perhaps, a maiden aunt. But more than likely she's closer to home — maybe a daughter, a wife and mother, a grandmother or a sister. She may work in an office, in a factory production line, in the public school system, at the corner grocery. She is not bound by lines of class distinction or educational level, race or religion.

What causes a woman to become a Lesbian? How can it be that two sisters, raised by the same parents in the same home, can turn in two different directions — one toward heterosexuality, the other toward homosexuality? Very simply, the answer is that no one knows. A great deal of research and study has been done in this country on the male homosexual, but very little has been done on the Lesbian. The reason for this, we suspect, lies in the status of women in our country. Because the male — masculinity — is so highly valued, it has been deemed to be imperative to search out the reasons for any deviation from this American norm. Also, the majority of persons working in research are men. Research on the Lesbian has, for the most part, been confined to women who were either psychiatric patients or in prison — which hasn't made for a very full or accurate picture.

Nevertheless, if you begin reading about the "causes" of homosexuality you will find that, as in the Bible, the answer you want to find will be somewhere. Each "expert" on the subject presents a different "cause." Our feeling, which is supported by a growing number of professional persons, is that homosexuality (in both men and women) is merely one dimension of the vastly complicated and varied spectrum of human sexuality. There has always been homosexuality; it has appeared in almost every culture in recorded history; it occurs in every species of animal.

Perhaps the most logical and least hysterical of all statements about homosexuality is the following made by Dr. Joel Fort, psychiatrist and public health specialist; Dr. Evelyn G.

Hooker, research psychologist at the University of California at Los Angeles; Dr. Joe K. Adams, psychologist and former mental health officer in California. The statement, made in August of 1966, is as follows:

> Homosexuals, like heterosexuals, should be treated as individual human beings, not as a special group, either by law or social agencies or employers.
>
> Laws governing sexual behavior should be reformed to deal only with clearly antisocial behavior, such as behavior involving violence or youth. The sexual behavior of individual adults by mutual consent in private should not be a matter of public concern.
>
> Some homosexuals, like some heterosexuals, are ill; some homosexuals, like some heterosexuals, are preoccupied with sex as a way of life. But probably for a majority of adults their sexual orientation constitutes only one component of a much more complicated life style. ...

Consider the stereotyped "box" most women in this country are placed in from birth: that of becoming wife and mother, nothing else. Consider then, the girl brought up in this box who finds her sexual identification to be Lesbian. How then express the "wife-and-mother" role? This conflict starts the process of self-searching which goes on for years and which for some is never resolved. ...

The art of motherhood in the human species is not instinctual. It is learned. ...

It simply does not follow, then, that every Lesbian is suffering untold qualms because she is frustrating her "natural" birthright for giving birth. There are many other ways for women to contribute creatively to society, and at this particular point in the history of the population of our globe, they may also be highly desirable. The Lesbian who does not feel frustrated because she doesn't have any children of her own may work in the teaching profession, she may be a playground director or a social worker who comes in contact with families and children. But the majority of Lesbians we have known have not expressed in any way the "void" they feel because they have no children. To the contrary, the expression, "I would prefer to lead a heterosexual life if I could," is much more apt to come from the male homosexual than from the female.

It must be said, however, that there are many Lesbians who are raising children — some successfully, some not so successfully. The rate of success is, of course, determined by the degree of self-acceptance and self-assurance of the mother and the permanence and stability of her relationship to her Lesbian partner. It takes guts, grit and determination. For if a mother is determined to be a Lesbian the courts will assume she is an "unfit mother" on the face of it and take her children away from her. It seems children must have the protection of heterosexuals, regardless. The fact that all homosexuals are products of heterosexuality seems to escape those who would judge the homosexual relationship.
...

The Quakers state: "Female homosexuality is free from the legal and, to a large extent, the social sanctions which are so important in the problems of male homosexuals." This is a myth that even the male homosexual has come to believe. It is true that in England there were never any laws pertaining to female homosexuality. But this is not true in the U.S.A. The Lesbian is just as subject to the sanctions of certain laws as the male homosexual; she is just as subject to arrest when she sets foot in a "gay bar," she is just as subject to blackmail and police harassment. The stigma attached to homosexuality has just as much effect on the Lesbian as she tries to deal with fear and society-imposed guilt in the problem areas of employment, family relationships and religion. Just because the record of arrests is so much smaller is no indication that the Lesbian is relatively free from legal or social sanction. It only means that she is less obvious and

less promiscuous. She has done a better job of covering up.
...

The most serious problem a Lesbian faces in life is that of self-acceptance. Like everyone else, she has been taught the cultural folklore that a Lesbian is something less than human — a sick, perverted, illegal, immoral animal to be shunned and despised. Needless to say, with the first glimmering of self-knowledge, of awareness that she has Lesbian tendencies, she becomes bogged down in doubt, fear, guilt and hostility. ...

Even when the Lesbian accepts her sexual identity and herself as a person, she still faces very real discrimination from society. If she has educated herself to a profession (a role doubly difficult for any woman) she can lose her professional status merely because someone points a finger. This is especially true of teachers, attorneys, doctors, social workers and other professions licensed by the state. But it can also be true for file clerks and secretaries. Very few employers are aware enough to realize that in the Lesbian he has an employee who must work, who will not get married or pregnant, who will devote her energies and capabilities to her job because she will always have to support herself. ... But the task of demythologizing, of education and redefinition of the homosexual is a long and arduous one.

A DOUBLE BIND

The Lesbian is in a double bind. She's discriminated against both as a Lesbian and as a woman. If she admits she's homosexual, she risks dismissal; and if she doesn't, she gets passed over for promotions she's qualified for on the grounds that she's likely to get married, get pregnant and leave.

Sociologist William Simon in "The Playboy Panel: Homosexuality," **Playboy**, April, 1971.

REVOLUTION AND CHANGE

The following exercise will explore your attitude toward change. Sometimes change brings progress, other times pain and suffering, and frequently both progress and human suffering are by-products of social, political, scientific, and technological change. Change can occur slowly or it can come suddenly and quickly (revolutionary change).

Consider each of the following circumstances carefully. Mark (G) whenever you feel gradual change is needed. Mark (R) for circumstances that you believe demand revolutionary change. And mark (S) if you think the status quo should be maintained (no change needed).

G = Gradual Change
R = Revolutionary Change
S = Status Quo

_____ 1. Legal procedures prohibiting same-sex marriages

_____ 2. Monogamy (traditional marriage laws and customs)

_____ 3. Sex education in the public schools

_____ 4. Job discrimination against gay people by the federal government

_____ 5. Any legal procedures prohibiting gay people from adopting children

_____ 6. Job discrimination against gay people by private employers

_____ 7. Existing divorce laws and customs

_____ 8. Laws preventing polygamy and polyandry

_____ 9. Housing discrimination against gay people

_____ 10. Military restrictions that prevent gay people from serving in the armed forces

_____ 11. Laws and customs preventing communal marriages

5 CHAPTER

SHOULD SEX
BE TAUGHT
IN PUBLIC
SCHOOLS?

Readings:

THE CASE FOR SEX EDUCATION

by National Congress of Parents and Teachers*

> This reading was prepared in 1969 by the President of the National Congress of Parents and Teachers, the PTA. The PTA is made up of almost 10 million parents, teachers, school administrators, and others interested in uniting the forces of home, school and community in behalf of children and youth. Its members belong to 40,198 local parent-teacher associations.

Reflect on the following questions as you read:

1. Why does the president of the PTA believe that sex education should be taught at school?
2. Why is home-school cooperation essential if sex education is to be taught successfully?
3. In the opinion of the president, what facts do the critics of sex education overlook?
4. How does the PTA react to the charge that sex education is a Communist plot?

*Elizabeth Hendryson, ''The Case for Sex Education,'' **PTA Magazine**, May, 1969, pp. 20-21. Reprinted with permission from the editor.

Like politics, national defense, and student unrest, sex education is an issue on which most of us have firm convictions. Nor do we feel any hesitation in expressing these convictions. And perhaps that is as it should be. All four of these subjects touch us closely, and yet all pose questions that are not capable of precise resolution. Hence we tend to believe that our opinion may well be just as valid as anyone else's, no matter what his credentials are.

On the other hand reason and incontrovertible evidence from the social sciences lead many of us to believe that sex education in the schools is not only desirable but necessary. Ideally the home should be the source of sound sex education, and for many children it is that. But what about the millions of children who for various reasons are either denied such education or receive miseducation on the subject?

Where but at school can we be sure of reaching these children and enabling them to gain the understanding and information on human sexuality that should be an essential part of every person's education? The children who are receiving sound sex education at home have nothing to fear or to lose from a rerun at school. Those who are not have a great deal to gain from a good sex education program in the school.

Over and over the PTA has expressed the belief that sound education about sexuality is basic if children are to understand human development, cope with the stresses and pressures of adolescence in modern America, and become adults capable of successful marriage and responsible parenthood. The goal of sex education, we believe, is to develop responsibility in human relations — relations between boys and girls, husband and wife, parents and children.

Of course parents have a major responsibility in this important area of education. Whether we parents are aware of it or not, from a child's earliest years we are imparting to him information and attitudes about sexuality — about what it means to be a boy or girl, a man or woman, a husband or wife, a parent. But important as this kind of teaching and learning is, it is not enough. And for "the more," many parents, even the best of parents, feel incompetent and inadequate. They feel ill prepared, factually or emotionally or both, to teach about sexual development, sex relations, and reproduction, with all their psychological, social, and ethical implications and consequences.

Hence the PTA has long advocated that public schools reinforce good home teaching, as well as help overcome the lack of or the wrong kind of teaching, by providing sex education or family life education — whatever one may choose to call it. It has urged a school role in such education because it has heard the pleas of parents for it. And parents, in their pleas for school help, have had the support of clergymen, physicians, nurses, and social workers who know well the damaging effects of sexual ignorance and lack of sexual ethics.

One of the lessons we have learned over the years is that the public schools are hard put to teach successfully what the community does not want, and in no area is this truer than that of sex education. Where such education has been ex-cellent, it is because the community wanted it and had a voice in deciding what was taught, and how, and when, and by whom . Here home-school cooperation is clearly essential. The most successful programs, I repeat, have come about through community understanding of the need and value of a sex education program and community participation in the development of its content and method.

When sex education was first introduced in the public schools, there was, as one might expect, opposition in some places from some people. These people objected that the school was usurping a responsibility that rightfully belongs to the home and the church. They ignored the fact that many churches provide no sex education or that if they do they want reinforcement from the school. They also ignored the fact that many homes provide no sound sex education what-ever and that many of these homes, like many churches, are eager for the schools to share this task. They disregarded still another fact — that rather than rushing into the sex education field, the schools entered it only after long and careful consideration. The truth is that public schools regard sex education not as their exclusive responsibility but as a responsibility shared with parents, religious institutions, and youth agencies.

Some people object to sex education per se; they believe that information provokes sexual curiosity and stimulates experimentation. The reverse is closer to reality. Ignorance is not a protection. Physicians and nurses report that many teenage girls have no idea how they become pregnant. And the curiosity of children and youth will not be denied or sup-pressed. When their questions are brushed aside or in-adequately answered by parents or teachers, children and youth will seek answers elsewhere — from each other or from older boys or girls. The answers they get may be false or dangerous. The answers may all too often be prefaced by the smirk or sneer that distorts whatever scraps of information may be forthcoming.

It is impossible to insulate children today from information and misinformation about sexuality. As Dr. Haim G. Ginott so cogently puts it in his ... book, **Between Parent and Teenager**: ''In words and pictures, our children are exposed to sex that is often sordid and vulgar. Our streets are a ceaseless source of misinformation. Smut peddlers never hesitate to share sex 'facts' and feelings. Precocious peers willingly tell of experiences, real and imagined.''

We cannot shut off children's access to newspapers, magazines, books, movies, television, and advertising. The mass media abound in stories, reports, and discussions of sex relations, sex ethics, venereal diseases, contraception, homosexuality. Some of the material is sober and responsible. Much of it is sensational, irresponsible, pornographic or verging on it. The question is not whether the community should provide sex education. The question is whether it is to be a scrap bag or a well-designed package. Unless we provide sound sex education by informed and responsible adults, the chances that our children will be miseducated rather than educated about human sexuality are dangerously high in our sex-oriented, sex-saturated society.

Hence the need for responsible sex education by trustworthy sources is imperative. This imperative need was recognized by the Congress of the United States when it authorized funds in Title III of the Elementary and Secondary Education Act to assist schools and communities in establishing or improving family life education from pre-school through adult levels.

With the need for sex education so obvious and so urgent, its provision by the public schools is now assailed by extremist groups. In the bulletin of the John Birch Society the society's founder and president calls for ''organized, nationwide, intensive, and angry and determined opposition'' to sex education in the public schools. Sex education, he charges, is a Communist plot to weaken the family, corrupt youth, and destroy the concept of morality.

The PTA response to this irrational attack must be nationwide and rational. We must back up our school boards and school administrators in resisting extremist pressures to abandon sex education. We must initiate intensive, nation-wide efforts to increase public understanding of the values and purposes of sex education and the crucial need for it. In our efforts we can count on the help of physicians, clergymen, nurses, social workers, family life specialists, educators, and many, many other persons concerned for the well-being of children and youth.

To strengthen family life, to increase self-understanding and self-respect, to develop sensitiveness in human relations, to build sexual and social responsibility, to enhance competence for responsible parenthood — this is what education about healthy human sexuality is designed to do. If America's children and youth are to be rightly educated in this crucial area of human responsibility, the PTA must forthrightly oppose any eliminations or weakening of sex education. We are committed to work for expansion and improvement of family life education and for home-school cooperation in providing it. Every child, we believe, has a need and a right to be educated for a responsible, happy family life.

OBJECTIVES OF SEX EDUCATION

1. To provide for the individual an adequate knowledge of his own physical, mental, and emotional maturation processes as related to sex.
2. To eliminate fears and anxieties relative to individual sexual development and adjustments.
3. To develop objective and understanding attitudes toward sex in all of its various manifestations — in the individual and in others.
4. To give the individual insight concerning his relationships to members of both sexes and to help him understand his obligations and responsibilities to others.
5. To provide an appreciation of the positive satisfaction that wholesome human relations can bring in both individual and family living.
6. To build an understanding of the need for the moral values that are essential to provide rational bases for making decisions.

7. To provide enough knowledge about the misuses and aberrations of sex to enable the individual to protect himself against exploitation and against injury to his physical and mental health.
8. To provide an incentive to work for a society in which such evils as prostitution and illegitimacy, archaic sex laws, irrational fears of sex, and sexual exploitation are nonexistent.
9. To provide the understanding and conditioning that will enable each individual to utilize his sexuality effectively and creatively in his several roles, e.g., as spouse, parent, community member, and citizen.

Sex Information and Education Council of the U.S.

93

SOME RESERVATIONS ABOUT SEX EDUCATION

by Mortimer Smith*

Mr. Smith is the Executive Director of the Council for Basic Education. The CBE is an organization of laymen, school board members, concerned parents, and others interested in strengthening the basic subjects in American schools. Its membership is approximately 3,300.

As you read try to answer the following questions:

1. What does the author feel is the basic issue in the sex education controversy?
2. What dangers does the author see in sex education programs?
3. The author believes that public schools do have a role to play in sex education. What is this role?

*Mortimer Smith, ''Some Reservations About Sex Education,'' **Parents**, November, 1969, pp. 66-67, 143. Reprinted with permission.

As far as educating and informing the young about sex, there were precious few attempts to do it in our grandparents' day. There was an occasional birds-and-bees lecture in the front parlor, embarrassing alike to the parent who gave the lecture and the child who was the recipient of it; as for including sex education in school programs, that was simply unthinkable.

Now we have gone to the other extreme. Although there have been modest programs of sex education in many schools for some time, during the last two or three years there has been a great expansion of such programs. The U.S. Office of Education is now supporting family life and sex education "as an integral part of the curriculum for pre-school to college and adult level."

A national organization with a distinguished board of directors, the Sex Information and Education Council of the U.S. (SIECUS) is urging cradle-to-college sex education and is very active in advising schools about appropriate programs.

I believe that the attempt to get away from hypocrisy about sex is a healthy and welcome development, and I hope we can discuss the issues in sex education usefully and constructively. Unfortunately the subject is already beclouded by some political extremists who claim that school sex education material such as that developed by SIECUS is un-American and part of "a filthy communist plot." This, of course, is nonsense. In fact, the official attitude toward sex in communist countries is extremely puritanical and repressive, quite contrary to the openness of discussion SIECUS and other such programs encourage.

But in any case, to discuss sex education in political terms is absurd. What is really at issue is whether or not such programs will promote the development in our children of a healthy and responsible attitude toward sex. ... I am fearful that the total immersion in sex education, making such teaching "a continuous process," as advocated by many, may simply add to that preoccupation with sex which the very proponents of these programs hope to counteract. We are running the risk of turning sex education into a holy crusade that promises more than it can deliver, that encourages us to believe that through sex education our children will gain total understanding and will develop, therefore, a reasonable and honest attitude toward sex.

What kind of information should young people acquire? How much understanding can they gain? One of the assumptions held by advocates of school sex education programs is that such teaching should begin in the kindergarten and earlier. We should provide information about sex to children of three to six years of age, they maintain, and convey to the children certain attitudes about sex; so they will understand that sex is a part of each of us, that the sex act does not always result in a baby, and that sexual intercourse is one of the most important aspects of the relationship that exist between a husband and wife.

Such teaching, it seems to me, is unnatural, premature, and bewildering — if not positively harmful — to a child. I think something can be said for adults ignoring any kind of formal sex education for youngsters up to the age of nine or ten, confining themselves, instead, to answering the child's questions frankly and briefly, telling him what he wants to know without giving more information than he can comprehend. Curiosity about sex among children of this age is not constant but fitful and occasional. The major preoccupation of children is not sex; they're more concerned with learning to get along with friends and with developing social and academic skills. They're busy learning so many things — often with difficulty and frustration — that it seems unwise to impose on them our own highly charged feelings about this most complex subject.

It is a different matter, of course, with older children whose interest in sex is high. They are ready for knowledge about sex, and parents and teachers have a responsibility to answer their need. I would be in favor of anatomical and biological knowledge integrated into academic subjects for pre-teen and teen-aged children. But I would be rather wary of the extensive discussion programs about masturbation, mainly because I think young people have an innate sense of privacy which makes them reluctant to share intimacies in groups. This, it seems to me, is as it should be. The advocates of sex education programs insist that biological knowledge isn't enough, that students need to discuss "total sexuality" and "what it is to be a man and what it is to be a woman." I think students can gain more insight into their own sexual feelings from reading great literature that illustrates the power of passion to enrich or destroy lives (**Anna Karenina** is a fine example of such a work) than they possibly can from classroom discussions specifically focused on sex.

Another proposition that I look on with a degree of skepticism is that if we do not install all-out programs of sex education we will be faced with rising youthful misbehavior. There is little evidence to suggest that sex education will prevent misconduct. If it was so, Sweden, the pioneer country in a "total immersion" kind of sex education, would be a utopia free of youthful conflicts. But that country has a high rate of abortions and illegitimate births, rapidly increasing juvenile deliquency and very high frequency of venereal infection among teenagers. Says Dr. Malcom Tottie of the Swedish National Board of Health: "Despite all our efforts to educate the young people (about VD) through lectures, brochures, and other means, they just don't seem to care."

SEX EDUCATION IS DANGEROUS

Classroom instruction in sex means that some children will be exposed to information too soon, while others may receive it later than desirable. It will embarrass many youngsters, cause callousness in others, and may provoke some to experiment. Moreover, continuous sex education, from kingergarten through high school, can create a dangerous obsession with sex in even a normal child.

Excerpted from **Sex Education in The Schools?** This pamphlet is distributed by the Movement to Restore Decency (Motorede), a national organization sponsored by the John Birch Society.

Many of Sweden's leading doctors are now beginning to realize that removing ignorance about sex without providing some firm guides to conduct does not produce social well-being. And since value judgements can accompany sex instruction when it is given at home, but the schools are reluctant to lay down moral imperatives, this raises a problem. Sex education specialists advocate opening up for discussion all sorts of problems and issues, but since they rightly feel that the teaching of values is the parents' job, they avoid suggesting any resolution of such problems and issues.

Still another debatable proposition is that the lack of formal sex education blights human development. At the risk of being regarded as a real fossil, I would say that this is not necessarily true. There are many men and women who were never given a word of instruction by parents or teachers and yet are reasonably, even happily, adjusted sexually. The idea that middle-aged people today who never discussed homosexuality or their erotic dreams with adults when they were teenagers are now repressed or prurient monsters is nonsense.

These, then, are some of the reservations I have about some current sex education programs. I am certainly not in favor of a conspiracy of silence regarding sex. Parents who feel comfortable doing so should inform their children as occasions naturally arise, about "the facts of life," and they should see that an interested youngster gets material to read which discusses the problems on his mind. ... Self learning through books and through conversations with contemporaries is a time-honored and often effective method of sex education. Gaining knowledge and wisdom about man's most intimate and private relationships does not depend on teacher-led group discussions. ...

This doesn't mean that the schools have no role as educators about sex. I see their role as a limited, fairly precise, one. I agree with Dr. John H. Moehle, retiring Superintendent of Carle Place Schools on Long Island, who is opposed to teaching sex as an isolated course but attempted in his school system to integrate instruction with the present curriculum. He says: "Units of sex information are taught

by trained teachers in the subject areas of health, biology, and home economics. These teachers fit the instruction into that part of the curriculum where it has natural meaning. If we are to teach more units of instruction of a specialized nature, interweaving the materials into academic subjects where they have natural association." ...

If communities decide that they want sex programs in the schools on the scale now being advocated by many specialists in the field, they must first consider whether or not such programs can be fitted into an already full schedule. The average eighth-grader is taking math, science, English, social studies, perhaps a foreign language, music, art, home economics, and physical education; he belongs to clubs, athletic teams, and has other extra-curricular interests.

Any sex-education programs we desire must be planned so as not to consume study time that the schools can ill afford to give up.

What I am pleading for in sex education is moderation, the golden mean.

EVALUATING SOURCES

A critical thinker must always question his various sources of information. Historians, for example, usually distinguish between primary sources (eyewitness accounts) and secondary sources (writings based on primary or eyewitness accounts, or other secondary sources). Most textbooks are examples of secondary sources. A diary written by a Civil War veteran is one example of a primary source. In order to be a critical reader one must be able to recognize primary sources. However, this is not enough. Eyewitness accounts do not always provide accurate descriptions. Historians may find ten different eyewitness accounts of an event and all the accounts might interpret the event differently. Then they must decide which of these accounts provide the most objective and accurate interpretations.

Test your skill in evaluating sources by participating in the following exercise. Pretend you are living 2000 years in the future. You have just run across an old magazine article while browsing in the library. It arouses your curiosity about the sex education controversy in American schools during the latter half of the 20th Century. Your teacher tells you to write an essay about this controversy. Consider carefully each of the following source descriptions. First, underline only those descriptions you feel would serve as primary sources assigning the number (1) to the most objective and accurate primary source, number (2) to the next most accurate and so on until the ranking is finished. Then discuss and compare your evaluations with other class members.

Assume that all of the following essays, articles, and books deal with the sex education controversy in America and its causes.

_____ 1. A letter to the editor of a metropolitan news-paper in 1980, written by a superintendent of schools

_____ 2. A book by President Nixon

_____ 3. The lecture notes for a sex education course taught in 1978

_____ 4. An article by Margaret Mead

_____ 5. An essay written by an English journalist in 1968

_____ 6. A political speech on sex education delivered by George Wallace in 1972

_____ 7. An essay by an American sociologist written in 1969

_____ 8. The results of a poll taken among public school teachers in 1976

_____ 9. The article in this chapter by Mortimer Smith

_____ 10. A 1965 New York Times newspaper editorial

_____ 11. A statement by the Sexual Freedom League released in 1965

_____ 12. A biography written in 2009 by someone who was a high school student during the 1970's

_____ 13. A sociology textbook written in 2053

ORGANIZATIONS TO CONTACT

American Education Lobby
20 E Street, N.W., Dodge House
Washington, D.C. 20001

American Institute of Family Relations
5287 Sunset Blvd.
Los Angeles, Calif. 90027

Basic Education
725 15th St., N.W.
Washington, D.C. 20005

Black Women's Liberation Committee
346 West 20th St.
New York, N.Y. 10011

Commission on Marriage and Family Life
475 Riverside Dr., Room 711
New York, N.Y. 10027

**Committee to Fight Exclusion of Homosexuals
    From the Armed Services**
3473½ Cahuenga Blvd.
Hollywood, Calif. 90068

Council on Equality for Homosexuals
Box 535
Peter Stuyvesant Station
New York, N.Y. 10009

Council on Religion and the Homosexual
330 Ellis St.
San Francisco, Calif. 94102

Daughters of Bilitis
141 Prince St.
New York, N.Y. 10012

Homosexual Information Center
3473½ Cahuenga Blvd.
Los Angeles, Calif. 90068

Lucy Stone League
133 East 58th St.
New York, N.Y. 10022

Mattachine Society, Inc.
348 Ellis St.
San Francisco, Calif. 94102

Men Our Masters / Women Our Wonders
1889 Jane St.
Wantagh, N.Y. 11793

National Catholic Conference on Family Life
c/o U.S. Catholic Conference
1312 Massachusetts Ave., N.W.
Washington, D.C. 20005

National Committee for Sexual Civil Liberties
18 Ober Rd.
Princeton, N.J. 08540

National Congress of Parents and Teachers
700 North Rush St.
Chicago, Ill. 60611

National Council on Family Relations
1219 University Ave., S.E.
Minneapolis, Minnesota 55414

National Education Association
1201 16th St. N.W.
Washington, D.C. 20036

National Organization for Women
P.O. Box 114 Cathedral Station
New York, N.Y. 10025

National Woman's Party
Belmont House
144 Constitution Ave., N.E.
Washington, D.C. 20002

Rene Guyon Society (sexual freedom)
324 First St.
Alhambra, Calif. 91802

Sex Information and Education Council of the U.S.
1855 Broadway
New York, N.Y. 10023

Sexual Freedom League
Box 14034
San Francisco, Calif. 94114

Student Homophile League
202 Earl Hall
Columbia University
New York, N.Y. 10027

WITCH (women's rights)
P.O. Box 694
Stuyvesant Station
New York, N.Y. 10009

ACKNOWLEDGMENTS

Illustration and Picture Credits

Page

2   Reprinted with permission from Doubleday and Co., Inc.

3   Reprinted with permission from **New Guard**

11   Reprinted with permission from Random House

16   United Press International Photo

26   Reprinted with permission from the **Chicago-Sun Times**. Editorial Cartoon by Jacob Burck.

48   Reprinted with permission from Association Press

75   Reprinted with permission from **The Minnesota Daily**

85   Reprinted with permission from Paul R. Hagen

87   Reprinted with permission from **National Review**, 150 East 35 Street, New York, N.Y. 10016

meet
the editors

GARY E. McCUEN, currently a social studies teacher at Eisenhower Senior High School in Hopkins, Minnesota, received his A.B. in history from Ripon College, and has an M.S.T. degree in history which he received from Wisconsin State University in Eau Claire, Wisconsin.

DAVID L. BENDER is a history graduate from the University of Minnesota. He also has an M.A. in government from St. Mary's University in San Antonio, Texas. He has taught social problems at the high school level and is currently working on additional volumes for the Opposing Viewpoints Series.